WHEN FISH

To Timothy and Petra

with love

Michael

Michael Boyle never did like facing up to decisions that were not likely to be popular, with other people as well as also with himself. As a result his choice of careers zig-zagged from merchant banker, or more accurately bank clerk, to removal man, lift operator, and Victoria Line underground construction worker before finally arriving, with parents now too exhausted to resist, at his original first choice – the theatre.

Five, highly enjoyable years followed before he emerged still not satisfied. More casting about and then twenty-three years at the civilised City and Guilds of London followed by a delicious two years of early retirement, before a late ten years of his supposed second love – teaching. All of it rewarding but not exactly the dream CV.

The one thing that has consistently returned to the centre of his values and his needs has been the story of Jesus and the whole legacy spawned by it. In this book, he attempts to articulate what it is that has made it and continues to make it so important to him.

WHEN FISHES FLEW?

Reconnecting with the Jesus stories

Michael Boyle

THE REAL PRESS
www.therealpress.co.uk

Published in 2021 by the Real Press.
www.therealpress.co.uk
© Michael Boyle

ISBN (print) 9781912119158
ISBN (ebooks) 9781912119141

Preface

This book is aimed at those who, like me, have had an impulse to explore the spiritual dimension of themselves, and have, nevertheless, given little time to do so.

My impulse was heightened by the wonderful introduction my father gave my sister and me to that side of ourselves - in our case through the Christian story; but love and truth are universal, and what significance is there in which language they are expressed?

As far as I am concerned, any religion, teaching, belief, philosophy, story, or way of life that has at its core unconditional love is a way to yourself, and, in the same place, God. The Christian message is full of unconditional love, and so is worthy to be explored simply from that point of view.

To engage with this project I read, probably for the first time, the whole of the New Testament, Acts, and Letters. The Jesus story has always held a very important position in my life, although regularly sidelined to allow me full scope for attention to my own thoughts and plans. This return to it was a guided tour, so to speak, with constant reference to others, for explanations, illustrations, or just their take on particular episodes or teachings.

My invitation now to fellow wanderers, past or only part, or completely non-readers, is to take the time to make a return, or a first visit to that story, a chapter or two a day perhaps – in my company for what it's worth, and to, hopefully, also glimpse – as I did – the inexpressible joy and fulfilment it offers everyone who makes it part of their life.

My feeling was that a single consecutive narrative threaded through all the accounts would lend itself best for that purpose, with the riches of the four complete gospels to be visited at the reader's leisure. Tracing that narrative, deciding which, when there was more than one, description of a particular event or teaching to choose, identifying a hopefully logical order for those events in the story, has been far the hardest part of the work.

The two Nativity accounts I have obviously quoted in full, and I have tried to include an account of all the stories and teachings recorded, with the exception of where a passing reference is made to a story that is one of many like that I do not feel adds greatly to the message already given – and also the one major account of a miracle differing so little from the description of another, that it seems to me to have a real possibility of being a duplication in the material available to the gospel writers, who I can well understand would not feel entitled to exclude any material they had before them.

My comments are offered as a companion reader – the thoughts or ideas prompted by particular teachings or parts of the story – to, in return, hopefully provoke a dialogue with your own reactions, including also on those passages on which I have had no comment to make.

The chapters I have divided this work into have no significance other than as a possible reading pattern, or the gathering together of a homogenous piece. If not found comfortable, they should simply be ignored.

Prologue

God has always been an enormously significant part of my life, even in the context of the sometimes protracted periods when banished from my thoughts and with my whole attention fixed on the, often desperate, pursuit of perceived physical, emotional, and material ends.

Perhaps the 'desperate' element of this pursuit was rooted in an inmost sense that nothing made sense in the end without God, along with a troubled instinct that, if God was included, all my own treasured aims and wishes would need to be fundamentally reviewed, likely abandoned.

All the same, I haven't done badly in keeping my own private objectives intact. For anyone who feels they have done a lot of running away from the calls in their life, I reckon I can give them a good run for their money. My own marathon has been some 78 years, without a lot of breaks. The hound of Heaven has kept pace behind me. Will I have enough courage, even now, to fully turn and embrace it? God only knows.

I was as close, I reckon, as a child, to God as I have ever been. This was thanks to the wonderful introduction my sister and I had from my father to the concept. Love is all that matters. God and through him, Jesus his life and teaching, is the ultimate expression of it. Without love there is nothing. With love everything is possible.

With this wonderful opening of the mind my childish heart opened too to Jesus. I remember, as a small boy at boarding school, being struck by the, to me, primitive ideas of most of my fellow pupils in their concept of God – mostly involving angry old men with very long beards – and their curiosity as to what I was doing for the sometimes three or four minutes I spent on my knees by my bed as opposed to their own 15 to 20 seconds.

It was this realisation that the introduction my sister and I had had from my father was not universally shared, indeed that there could be people who have not ever even encountered a Christian or any other religious or spiritual story, that partly impelled me to want to share, with any who wish to take it up, the blessing I had received.

Another reason was my refusal to accept that the many non-believer, both agnostic and positive atheistic, friends I have, do not have a spiritual dimension to their life – a dimension that I call God, but they may have some different perception of.

For me, we are informed and pushed in our daily life by impulses from the depths of ourselves with which we are not in conscious direct contact, and which, in our conscious mind, we may struggle to articulate, or push aside to concentrate on a course of action we have in our conscious mind decided on. The source of those impulses, for me, is our true self. Most of us do not give a lot of time to spend with that self but count on our conscious mind, sometimes influenced by the impulses, to steer us roughly in the direction we wish to go.

I believe, for true happiness and fulfilment, we need to be in full contact with our full selves; and that involves time. If you want to get to the bottom of your heart you have to set aside time specifically for that purpose.

A thousand books have been written on contemplation, but basically the chatter of your conscious mind has to be patiently pushed back until you can start to descend deeper and deeper into yourself, where words start to cease to be the language of your experience. The stilling of one's busy mind is not an easy process and most journeys probably only succeed in going part of the way. Perhaps only one in ten comes near that deepest inner core. For me that's where God is, and the journey there is what I call praying.

Michael Ramsey, Archbishop of Canterbury, was once asked how long he prayed each day. 'About 2 minutes' he said. When the interviewer expressed surprise at this, Michael Ramsey added: 'But it usually takes me 28 minutes to get there.'

It sounds quick to me, but it's still too long as far

as I am concerned at this point in time. I think it's important to have a time limit in a regular pattern adopted. The 15 minutes Metropolitan Anthony Bloom advocates for 'knitting before the face of God' (see later) sounds about right to me as regards time. We have the important business of living as human beings to get on with as well after all.

I don't believe non-believers fail to make that journey. They just don't find God at the end of it. For me, the true self in the depths of our hearts cannot, in essence, be anything but Love, and that's what God is and that's how he is already in the depths of our hearts, waiting for a visit.

There is of course a huge range in the degrees of involvement of those who would wish to be called believers in God, from those, like St Francis, who have utterly given their lives to the service of communion with that God and their heart, to those who are unwilling to totally give up the link with the concept they were instructed in as children, perhaps for mainly cultural reasons, manifested in a visit to a church perhaps once a year, or in an instinctive desire to assemble in a place of worship at times of celebration, bereavement, or deepest crisis, but for whom otherwise the concept has little impact in their conscious lives.

Where do I come in this spectrum of commitment? As you may anticipate from my earlier reference, the most favourable description I can give is a pretty pathetic sometime follower with aspirations to be a disciple, who can still go for weeks, if not months, so pre-occupied with my worldly aims and anxieties that I venture not an inch below my conscious mind, who then, unfailingly, find myself, in due course, stranded in a sterile desert starving for some spiritual communion.

I have used the word 'believe' a number of times. I do not, though, to the annoyance of my agnostic and atheist friends, find it an appropriate word to describe my situation. If you have experienced love, (not referring, terrific though that is, to sexual passion) then it is not appropriate to describe your attitude to it as 'believing' in it. You have experienced it. It is. So, from my visits to my inmost core, I have experienced what I call the presence of God. It is no longer a question of belief. Faith may still be required at periods of particular bleakness and wilderness where there appears also to be nothing at the bottom of your heart, where you can only cling onto the knowledge that your past experience has happened, and the belief, yes then, that it still is, and will return.

I am lucky not to have experienced anything so bad, but CS Lewis has vividly described such moments in his despair after his wife died, hammering, as he put it, on the closed and locked doors that he had found at God's dwelling place, to hear only the sound of heavy bolts being shot into place on the other side, or Christ's call from the cross: 'My God, my God, why have you forsaken me?'

Even when love abandons you, and you cannot even be sure you still feel it yourself, can you doubt that it exists?

In the same way, I am unmoved by the challenges issued to the Christian story and the attempted ridicule poured onto it by sceptics. It is the most beautiful story I know and I am ready to accept and defend every word of it. At the same time, I do not depend on it for the experience I have had of God and Christ in my life. The story prompted and accompanied me on my journey into my heart and brought about my encounter there. If now evidence was unearthed to show a very different or even non-existent Jesus, it would not make a jot of difference. Christ is overwhelming love, and as such I have found him in my heart.

At the same time, I issue a counter challenge to the challengers. No, you can search Roman records in vain for any reference to Jesus, Pontius Pilate, or any of the turbulent events in Palestine described in the Gospels. There is one passing mention of a 'Christus' without further elaboration. But the phenomenon of Christianity itself is a fact – how teachings to and the experience of a tiny handful of humble people in a remote and insignificant corner of the mighty Roman Empire grew, first, across that empire to take it over and become its official religion, and then to spread across the world so that today, 2,000 years later, those teachings and the story of how they came to be delivered are to be found in every part of the globe, with followers continuing to be prepared to die in their service.

Those teachings came from someone. If not Jesus, who then was it, and how was it those humble people who received them were then inspired to have the will and courage to leave their homes and devote and risk the rest of their lives to carry their message across the world?

Something extraordinary happened. Surely no one can query that? Why should it not be the story as told and referred to in the near contemporary writings of the gospels, the Acts of the Apostles and St Paul's letters?

What is the explanation of the phenomenal impact those teachings and their accompanying story has had, when there were already many enlightened teachings and philosophies available in the ancient world, overlapping in many places with the Christian teachings?

My explanation is that the teachings and the life described with them accorded with and gave access to total fulfilment of the nature and aspirations of the human spirit; not part but total access. Of course what we do with that access is quite a different matter. We are human with human failings, and unless we are St Francis-like we are unlikely to have

11

the courage, energy, and unselfishness to have that access permanently central to our lives.

The promptings of flesh, weakness, cowardice, inertia, and pure laziness will constantly make themselves felt. Yet the access is there permanently, for us to reconnect with our truest selves..

I love the way the gospels differ from each other in their accounts of the same events – stories in one that are not in another, or the same story told differently, sometimes markedly, sometimes by just little descriptive variations. Four accounts by different people, written at different times for different purposes, using probably numerous different sources – some to simply tell the story, others to focus primarily on the teachings and their interpretations. It has the ring of truth and fits perfectly with the scenario.

In the exaltation of their newly discovered certainty, after the extraordinary events that followed the terrible shock of Jesus' death and removal from them, that, though not still physically with them, Jesus is still alive and with them in spirit, the disciples seize on the words he had spoken about his coming again in glory at the end of the world to bring about the kingdom of God.

In that exaltation, they assume that that return is imminent. They throw themselves with thrilling abandon into living the message of his teachings. Private possessions and property are pooled or sold for the common good so as to live together in community where each one seeks only what they need, and the needs of others are their primary concern; the ultimate expression of the communist ideal. They themselves will almost certainly all have had some personal contact with Jesus, and they are surrounded on all sides by those who were his most intimate disciples and followers. Why do they need to write down anything he said or did? They know it all by heart, and if they have a momentary memory lapse they have only to ask any of their neighbours. Anyway Christ himself will be back with them any time now, perhaps next week.

It is only when the months turn into years that perceptions start to change. The ideal of living together in a community was perhaps the first to go. That ideal of sharing everything, no personal possessions, of having only what you need is inspirational but difficult to maintain if some in the community are perceived as not being quite so sharing as others.

Living in a community is a very demanding discipline. Only a minority are suited to and can manage it – for example, some religious or monastic orders. It remains an ideal, though, the 'magnetic north' I once heard a preacher (Rev John Pridmore) refer to in respect of Christianity as a whole. Gradually, perhaps, the majority of those first members came to the conclusion that they would have to try to live that ideal individually in their own homes

After ten years, a new generation are growing up who have never personally seen or known Jesus. They need to be told of his life, his message, his teachings. Still on all sides are people who had personally known him who can be referred to. One can imagine, though, that the instruction of those children would have started to vary considerably depending on the memories of those instructing them.

Only after twenty years or so have passed do alarm bells start to ring. Perhaps Jesus was not going to return in any of their lifetimes. His closest followers and associates are beginning to die off. The variations in the stories told about him were probably growing wider and wider. There was a need to get down a full account of his life and teachings while there were still people who could be referred to who had witnessed that life and heard those teachings first hand.

This is perhaps where individual recollections started to get written down, but still not centrally organised or co-ordinated. Only after around fifty years does the first gospel, attempting a full statement of Jesus' life come to be written, followed by the others. Each of them, though, has its own objectives – some giving priority to the simple telling of the story, others primarily focussed on conveying the teachings and their interpretations with particular attention given to those events that could illustrate these.

It is unlikely that any of the gospels was written by an apostle. Each of the writers possibly had different sources hearing different versions of the same story, with different shadings. If the gospel accounts had been identical, I would have found it highly suspicious.

The church and other well-meaning bodies and associations appoint themselves arbiters and interpreters of that life and teaching, and directors of their followers, sometimes extremely helpfully and supportively, at other times precisely the opposite. Inevitably other people will not always get it right as far as we, personally, are concerned, and the moment you create a bureaucracy to deal with affairs of the spirit you're in trouble. How many angels, indeed, can you get on the head of a pin?

In the end we each of us have to make our journey ourselves. If, however, you're like me, and self–discipline to set aside the time, and steadfastness of spirit, do not come naturally or easily, then to do it with the company and leadership of a church can be very helpful.

Praying is one area where other people's wisdom has been critically important to me. Until my mind had been opened to that descent inside yourself, I think my prayers had been truer as a small boy, but then, even taking the time for pushing back pre-occupations of the mind and for finding the stillness in which contemplation becomes possible, the un-busyness and the stillness do not always follow.

For people like me it is perhaps only one time in ten we come anywhere near Archbishop Ramsey's wonderful two minutes. It is hardly surprising. You would not expect to undertake an equivalent physical feat without regular training. Why should you expect to do so mentally without the same degree of preparation and focus?

Metropolitan Anthony Bloom's 'School for Prayer' gives some enormously helpful insights on prayer, from which I quote later on.

It was at St Martin's, though, that I first returned to churchgoing and first discovered prayer arising from contemplation, as practised by all the clergy there, after, for me, a long and sterile absence which followed five years of school chapel every day and twice on Sundays, with a litany, lovely as it was, that I could have recited, without prompt, in any direction you liked.

It was there too that I came to understand that prayer can take place anywhere, at a bus stop, while you're dressing, for a period of any length – 20 seconds, a couple of minutes – it simply depends on your mind being open for it.

In particular, I have Rev Austen Williams to thank, in the last 10 years of his 27-year ministry at

St Martin's, for – among so many other examples of how practically, unsentimentally, and realistically to daily live the Christian word – introducing me through his example of praying to the beginning of an understanding. He used to say that when he prayed for someone, he first of all pictured them in his mind, and then he surrounded them with what he described as 'an act of imagining love' and then just held them there.

And he used to say in that act we came perhaps as close to the nature of God as we could ever hope to be.

It was at St Martin's too that I was introduced to the concept that it was alright to fail. There is a lovely part of Bunyan's Pilgrim's progress that describes the wicket gate that leads onto the journey to God. The gate is lit by a flickering light above, which comes and goes when viewed from a distance. The St Martin's clergy used to meet for breakfast together and would ask each other how the flickering light was that day. 'Not too bad'. 'Pretty faint'. 'Not a sign'. If you failed, you did not think too much about it. Sufficient unto the day.... You simply came back to have another go next day.

In 'School for Prayer', Metropolitan Anthony Bloom delightfully describes how, as a newly ordained Russian Orthodox priest, he was assigned over Christmas as a chaplain to an old people's home, and was summoned by an old lady looking for guidance on how to pray. For years, she said, she had been asking people who were reputed to know about prayer, all to no avail, so she thought that, as he probably knew nothing, he might have blundered onto the right answer. "An encouraging situation," he says!

So he asked what the problem was. For fourteen years, she said, she had been praying the Jesus prayer almost continuously, and never had she perceived God's presence at all. So, he said, he blundered out with the first thing in his mind. "If you speak all the time, you don't give God a chance to place a word in."

He prescribed something different. After breakfast she should go to her room and arrange it so that it was pleasant to be in. Then she should choose her favourite chair, sit in it, and just take stock of where she was. Then she should take her knitting and for fifteen minutes just "knit before the face of God", during which time he forbade her to say one word of prayer.

After some time, she came to see him and said: "It works!"

"What works? What happens?" he said, as he was extremely curious to know. So she described how after breakfast she put her room in order so that there was nothing to distract her. Then she sat in her chair and thought: "Oh how lovely. I have fifteen minutes in which I can do nothing without feeling guilty." And then she looked around and for the first time in years realised what a nice room she lived in. Then she remembered she had to knit before the face of God, so she took up her knitting and began to knit. The click of the needles and the ticking of the clock were the only sounds, which just highlighted the otherwise surrounding silence, a silence which she began to perceive was not just an absence of noise, but that the silence had substance.

It was not an absence of something but a presence of something. It began to pervade her and come to meet the silence in her, and then she said: "All of a sudden I perceived that the silence was a presence. At the heart of the silence there was Him who is all stillness, all peace, all poise."

This reminds me of the time I asked Ven Trevor Nash, who was about to lead a retreat I had signed up for, whether it would be a good idea for me to bring a book with me. He thought for a moment and then he said "No. There's no harm in doing a bit of sitting still to the glory of God."

By the time of Christ, many philosophical ideas had already been put forward in the Roman world that, again, are cardinal features of the Christian teaching, including the concept of Love your Enemy. How could it have been otherwise? Life must always have had the same fundamental ingredients, the same treasure at its heart with some species evolving a greater consciousness of. I believe that treasure is present in every expression of life, sometimes, indeed, never to be visibly seen.

But consider the astonishing demonstrations of love from wild animals to those of another species, including humans, defying all the 'natural' limits ascribed to their natures by scientific study. The joy of Christian the Lion, returned as a young adult to his natural habitat, when reunited years later in the wild with the two young men who had brought him up as a cub. The fully grown hippo, constantly, in its urgent desire to be near them, clambering onto and breaking the bed of the couple who had rescued her as an orphan.

The dove that refused to allow its cat friend the right to a catnap, constantly cooing into an upturned ear, and when gently batted to one side by a sleepy paw, returning to coo even more vigorously into the other ear. The family of completely wild, and originally labelled dangerous, elephants who came to pay their respects when the reserve owner who had saved them from culling, and whom they had come to regard as a friend, died.

When it comes to humans, exquisite pieces of prehistoric art establish their creators as possessing every bit of consciousness and sensitivity we claim today. How could we imagine such people not having the same access to the depths of their inner selves that we have? Harder no doubt, beset, daily probably, with life and death struggles for survival, with no example to encourage or guide them, pre-Buddha, pre-Christ pre every teaching. The same truths, though, were there to be discovered, the same journeys to be made, the same rendezvous with themselves and God. I feel lucky to have been born after Christ's example of how to access that true self and how to live your life so that you stay in communion with that self and God.

Were cavemen any less the children of God? Why were they deprived of the advantages we have? You can only hear what you are ready to hear. The great teachers perhaps came at the first moment they would be heard, or perhaps, more likely, the ages regularly threw up great visionaries and thinkers whose insights and visions, without the existence of inter-society communication, died with them and the probably tiny circle of people they had been shared with.

As regards miracles, my difficulty was not with the events themselves. I do not feel qualified to rule out wonders. My problem was their purpose and their randomness. Why here and not there? Why not everywhere? My difficulty was solved by Geoffrey Brown's reference to them in a sermon at St Martin-in-the-Fields. 'Sacraments of love to a pilgrim people' – not solutions to all our problems, but signals of the infinite love available for people trying to find their way to themselves and God.

Jesus, full of God's overwhelming love, simply

could not stop himself pouring it out onto everyone who asked for it, with their being healed in consequence; later continued by his disciples when they came to realise that they were meant, themselves, to carry on his work.

To those who point to the increasing scientific discovery that the whole shape of our natures and the full spectrum of our emotions are rooted in a series of chemicals in the brain, I say: "Of course!' If, as Christians and other religious followers believe, life was created by a divine power from which our human form evolved, for the purposes, when we should be ready, of self-discovery and reunion with that divine power, then obviously that human form must come supplied with all the ingredients and tools to make that possible.

The chemicals are there for a purpose. Why else would they have developed? They allow us to experience every emotion and, naturally responding to and supplying the appropriate stages of real contemplation and mental focus, they enable vision, inspiration, and revelation. The discovery that they could be independently stimulated by drugs and to a lesser degree alcohol has meant that the states of mind they create are regularly experienced, not as aids and enablers towards self understanding and the journey to one's core, but as artificial stimulative experiences for their own sake.

It may be argued that there is nothing much

wrong with this. If we have these experiences within us why should we not access them at will? I think the same situation applies to them as to sexual experience. Nothing much wrong with a bit of masturbation there you could say; but a bit sad if it comes to replace the real thing. The same with the mental and emotional masturbation of drugs.

An incidental thought – I wonder if a person referring to an LSD trip would describe the visions they had experienced as real or figments of their imagination?

I believe that in its myriad random forms of expression, all life remains unshakeably part of divine creation. It would be a brave person indeed who would try to articulate God's purpose in the context of something like the Holocaust, or illness, or simple natural disasters. But I do believe at the end all things will be well and all manner of things will be well.

There are many examples quoted of the momentary experiences of people who have clinically died and been revived, most involving travelling towards an overwhelmingly bright light; hinted at, too, for me, in the whispered words put into the mouth of Mel Ferrer playing the dying Prince Andre in the Hollywood production of War and Peace – "It's so easy. It's so easy" – or the real words of the dying Hollywood mogul Louis B. Mayer: "Nothing matters. Nothing matters" – the wonderful irrelevance of the brightest brightness we can muster, like turning on a torch on a glorious summer day in the garden.

What is the purpose? The only thing I find worth quoting is the wonderful words of Bono: "All we're doing really is just helping each other home."

Would my faith sustain me in the event of apocalypse and the collapse of civilisation? I have serious doubts. But one thing I am certain of. It would never be more needed, to prevent us from becoming ravening animals.

Author's plea

The purpose of this book is to try to persuade people who have not in a long time or never done so, to look or to look again contemplatively at the New Testament story. Just over half of the book is devoted, therefore, to tracing a single consecutive narrative of that story through the four gospels, the Acts of the Apostles, and Paul's letters.

The other half consists of, first, a statement of my personal starting point with the story, which you have just read, and then my passing comments relating to the impact on me, and my understanding of various passages from it. These comments, however, are only companionable asides in a shared read. Their most profitable product will be the prompting of the fellow reader to contemplate their own reactions, particularly, in fact, in relation to those passages on which I did not feel I had a comment worth making.

It is the full reading of the New Testament passages that this book is about. So if readers are tempted to skip these to get, out of curiosity, to the comments, the book will have failed in its purpose.

The plea then is to use the book as it was intended. A reading pattern of, say, a chapter or two a day would take you on a three week or so journey through the whole amazing story.

THE STORY

Chapter I
Birth of John and the Nativity

Luke   1. 5 - 2.21   (RSV)
Matthew 1.18 - 2.12   (RSV)

Luke 1

5   In the days of Herod, King of Judea, there was a priest named Zechariah, of the division of Abijah; and he had a wife of the daughters of Aaron and her name was Elizabeth.   6   And they were both righteous before God, walking in all the commandments and ordinances of the Lord blameless.   7   But they had no child, because Elizabeth was barren, and both were advanced in years.

8   Now while he was serving as priest before God when his division was on duty,   9   according to the custom of the priesthood, it fell to him by lot to enter the temple of the Lord and burn incense.   10   And the whole multitude of the people were praying outside at the hour of incense.   11   And there appeared to him an angel of the Lord standing on the right side of the altar of incense.   12   And

Zechariah was troubled when he saw him, and fear fell upon him. 13 But the angel said to him "Do not be afraid Zechariah, for your prayer is heard, and your wife Elizabeth will bear you a son, and you shall call his name John.

14 And you will have joy and gladness, and many will rejoice at his birth;

15 for he will be great before the Lord,
and he shall drink no wine nor strong drink,
and he will be filled with the Holy Spirit,
even from his mother's womb.

16 And he will turn many of the sons of Israel to the Lord their God,

17 and he will go before him in the spirit and power of Elijah,
to turn the hearts of the fathers to the children
and the disobedient to the wisdom of the just,
to make ready for the Lord a people prepared"

18 And Zechariah said to the angel, "How shall I know this? For I am an old man and my wife is advanced in years" 19 and the angel answered him "I am Gabriel, who stand in the presence of God; and I was sent to speak to you, and to bring you this good news. 20 And behold, you will be silent and unable to speak until the day that these things come to pass, because you did not believe my words, which will be fulfilled in their time". 21 And the people were waiting for Zechariah, and they wondered at his delay in the temple. 22 And when

he came out, he could not speak to them, and they perceived that he had seen a vision in the temple; and he made signs to them and remained dumb. 23 And when his time of service was ended, he went to his home.

24 After these days his wife Elizabeth conceived, and for five months she hid herself, saying 25 "Thus the Lord has done to me in the days when he looked at me, to take away my reproach among men".

26 In the sixth month the angel Gabriel was sent from God to a city of Galilee named Nazareth, 27 to a virgin betrothed to a man whose name was Joseph, of the house of David; and the virgin's name was Mary. 28 And he came to her and said, "Hail, oh favoured one, the Lord is with you" 29 but she was greatly troubled at the saying and considered in her mind what sort of greeting this might be. 30 And the angel said to her, "Do not be afraid, Mary for you have found favour with God. 31 And behold you will conceive in your womb and bear a son and you shall call his name Jesus.

32 He will be great, and will be called the Son of the Most High:

and the Lord God will give to him the throne of his father David,

33 and he will reign over the house of Jacob for ever;

and of his kingdom there will be no end."

34 And Mary said to the angel, "How shall this be, since I have no husband?"

35 And the angel said to her

"The Holy Spirit will come upon you,

and the power of the Most High will overshadow you;

therefore the child to be born will be called holy,

the Son of God

36 And behold, your kinswoman Elizabeth in her old age has also conceived a son; and this is the sixth month with her who was called barren. 37 For with God nothing will be impossible". 38 And Mary said "Behold, I am the handmaid of the Lord; let it be to me according to your word". And the angel departed from her.

39 in those days Mary arose and went with haste to the hill country, to a city of Judah, 40   and she entered the house of Zechariah and greeted Elizabeth.

41 And when Elizabeth heard the greeting of Mary, the babe leapt in her womb; and Elizabeth was filled with the Holy Spirit 42 and she exclaimed with a loud cry, "Blessed are you among women, and blessed is the fruit of your womb! 43 And why is this granted me, that the mother of my Lord should come to me? 44 For behold, when the voice of your greeting came to my ears, the babe in my womb leapt for joy. 45 And blessed is she who believed that there would be a fulfilment of what was spoken

to her from the Lord."

46 And Mary said

"My soul magnifies the Lord,

47 and my spirit rejoices in God my saviour,

48 for he has regarded the low estate of his handmaiden.

For behold, henceforth all generations will call me blessed;

49 for he who is mighty has done great things for me

and holy is his name

50 and his mercy is on those who fear him
from generation to generation.

51 He has shown strength with his arm,

he has scattered the proud in the imagination of their hearts,

52 he has put down the mighty from their thrones,
and exalted those of low degree;

53 he has filled the hungry with good things,
and the rich he has sent empty away.

54 He has helped his servant Israel,
in remembrance of his mercy,

55 as he spoke to our fathers,
to Abraham and to his posterity for ever"

56 and Mary remained with her about three months, and returned to her home.

57 Now the time came for Elizabeth to be delivered, and she gave birth to a son.

58 And her neighbours and kinsfolk heard that the

Lord had shown great mercy to her, and they rejoiced with her. 59 And on the eighth day they came to circumcise the child; and they would have named him Zechariah after his father, 60 but his mother said, "Not so; he shall be called John." 61 And they said to her," None of your kindred is called by this name." 62 And they made signs to his father, enquiring what he would have him called. 63 And he asked for a writing tablet, and wrote, "His name is John." And they all marvelled. 64 And immediately his mouth was open and his tongue loosed and he spoke, blessing God. 65 And fear came on all their neighbours. And all these things were talked about through all the hill country of Judea; 66 and all who heard them laid them up in their hearts, saying, "What then will this child be?" For the hand of the Lord was with him.

67 And his father Zechariah was filled with the Holy Spirit, and prophesied saying

68 "Blessed be the Lord God of Israel for he has visited and redeemed his people,

69 and has raised up a horn of salvation for us
   in the house of his servant David,

70 as he spoke by the mouth of his holy prophets from of old,

71 that we should be saved from our enemies,
   and from the hand of all who hate us;

72 to perform the mercy promised to our fathers,
   and to remember his holy covenant,

73 the oath which he swore to our father Abraham,
74 to grant us

   that we, being delivered from the hand of our
enemies,

   might serve him without fear,

75 in holiness and righteousness before him all the
days of our life.

76 And you, child, will be called the prophet of the
Most High;

   for you will go before the Lord to prepare his
ways,

77 to give knowledge of salvation to his people
   in the forgiveness of their sins,

78 through the tender mercy of our God
   When the day shall dawn upon us from on high

79 to give light to those who sit in darkness and in
the shadow of death,

   to guide our feet into the way of peace."

80 And the child grew and became strong in spirit,
and he was in the wilderness till the day of his
manifestation to Israel.

Luke 2

In those days a decree went out from Caesar
Augustus that all the world should be enrolled.

2 This was the first enrolment, when Quirinius was
governor of Syria.

3 And all went to be enrolled, each to his own city.

4 And Joseph also went up from Galilee, from the

city of Nazareth, to Judea, to the city of David, which is called Bethlehem, because he was of the house and lineage of David, 5 to be enrolled with Mary, his betrothed, who was with child. 6 And while they were there, the time came for her to be delivered. 7 And she gave birth to her first-born son and wrapped him in swaddling clothes, and laid him in a manger, because there was no place for them in the inn.

8 And in that region there were shepherds out in the field, keeping watch over their flock by night.

9 And an angel of the Lord appeared to them, and the glory of the Lord shone around them, and they were filled with fear. 10 And the angel said to them, "Be not afraid; for behold, I bring you good news of a great joy which will come to all the people; 11 for to you is born this day in the city of David a saviour, who is Christ the Lord. 12 And this will be a sign for you: You will find a babe wrapped in swaddling clothes and lying in a manger." 13 And suddenly there was with the angel a multitude of the heavenly host praising God and saying

14 Glory to God in the highest,
    and on earth peace among men with
    whom he is pleased!"

15 When the Angels went away from them into heaven, the shepherds said to one another, "Let us go over to Bethlehem and see this thing that has happened, which the Lord has made known to us." 16 And they went with haste, and found Mary and

Joseph and the babe lying in a manger. 17 And when they saw it they made known the saying which had been told them concerning this child; 18 And all who heard it wondered what the shepherds told them. 19 But Mary kept all these things, pondering them in her heart. 20 And the shepherds returned, glorifying and praising God for all they had heard and seen, as it had been told them.

Matthew

1. 18   Now the birth of Jesus Christ took place in this way. When his mother Mary had been betrothed to Joseph, before they came together she was found to be with child of the Holy Spirit; 19 and her husband Joseph, being a just man and unwilling to put her to shame, resolved to divorce her quietly. 20 But as he considered this, behold an angel of the Lord appeared to him in a dream saying "Joseph son of David do not fear to take Mary your wife, for that which is conceived in her is of the Holy Spirit; 21 she will bear a son, and you shall call his name Jesus, for he will save his people from their sins", 22 All this took place to fulfil what the Lord had spoken by the prophet: 23 "Behold, a virgin shall conceive and bear a son

and his name shall be called Emmanuel"

(which means, God with us). 24 When Joseph woke from sleep he did as the angel of the Lord commanded him; he took his wife, 25 but knew her not until she had borne a son; and he called his name Jesus.

Matthew 2

Now when Jesus was born in Bethlehem of Judea in the days of Herod the king, behold, wise men from the East came to Jerusalem saying, 2 " Where is he who has been born king of the Jews? For we have seen his star in the East and have come to worship him". 3 When Herod the king heard this, he was troubled, and all Jerusalem with him; 4 and assembling all the chief priests and scribes of the people he enquired of them where the Christ was to be born. 5 They told him, "In Bethlehem of Judaea; for so it is written by the Prophet:

6 'And you, oh Bethlehem in the land of Judah,

    are by no means least among the rulers of Judah;

       for from you shall come a ruler

       who will govern my people Israel'"

7 Then Herod summoned the wise men secretly and ascertained from them what time the star appeared; 8 and he sent them to Bethlehem, saying, "Go and search diligently for the child, and when you have found him bring me word, that I too may come and worship him". 9 When they had heard the king they went their way; and lo, the star which they had seen in the East went before them, till it came to rest over

the place where the child was. 10 When they saw the star, they rejoiced exceedingly with great joy; 11 and going into the house they saw the child with Mary his mother, and they fell down and worshipped him. Then, opening their treasures, they offered him gifts, gold and frankincense and myrrh. 12 And being warned in a dream not to return to Herod, they departed to their own country by another way.

This is the most beautiful story I know. One can't help speculating – Was there a comet in the sky at the time – like the fascinating appearance, as scheduled, of Halley's comet in the 1980s – a signal to the ancient world of the advent of something of great significance? Like the monks in their search for a new Dalai Lama, did wise men set out to try and find the answer to this great mystery?

The sublime Shepherds story – how could it be possible for something so momentously joyful as Christ's birth to come about without manifestations of it?

Chapter II
Simeon

Luke 2. 22 – 35   (RSV)

22   And when the time came for their purification according to the law of Moses, they brought him up to Jerusalem to present him to the Lord 23 (as it is written in the law of the Lord, "Every male that opens the womb shall be called holy to the Lord") 24 and to offer a sacrifice according to what is said in the law of the Lord," a pair of turtle doves, or two young pigeons".

25   Now there was a man in Jerusalem, whose name was Simeon and this man was righteous and devout, looking for the consolation of Israel, and the Holy Spirit was upon him.   26   And it had been revealed to him by the Holy Spirit that he should not see death before he had seen the Lord's Christ. 27 And inspired by the Spirit he came into the temple; and when the parents brought in the child Jesus to do for him according to the custom of the law, 28 he took him up in his arms and blessed God and said

29   "Lord now lettest thou thy servant depart in peace,

according to thy word;

30 for mine eyes have seen thy salvation

31 which thou hast prepared in the presence of all peoples,

32 a light for revelation to the Gentiles, and for glory to thy people Israel."

33 And his father and his mother marvelled at what was said about him;

34 and Simeon blessed them and said to Mary his mother

"Behold , this child is set for the fall and rising of many in Israel,

and for a sign that is spoken against

35 (and a sword will pierce through your own soul also),

that thoughts out of many hearts may be revealed."

It's a lovely idea, this holy old man who has felt intimations that he will somehow see the Christ, God's saviour of the world, before he dies; realising as he takes the baby in his arms that this is the moment, giving rise to the utterance of the beautiful words, now known as the Nunc Dimittis, repeated in so many of our services.

The Flight to Egypt and the Slaughter of the Innocents

Matthew 2. 13 – 18 (RSV)

13 Now when (the wise men) had departed, behold, an angel of the Lord appeared to Joseph in a dream and said, "Rise, take the child and his mother, and flee to Egypt, and remain there till I tell you; for Herod is about to search for the child, to destroy him." 14 And he rose and took the child and his mother by night, and departed to Egypt, 15 and remained there until the death of Herod. This was to fulfil what the Lord had spoken by the prophet, "Out of Egypt have I called my son."

16 Then Herod, when he saw that he had been tricked by the wise men, was in a furious rage, and he sent and killed all the male children in Bethlehem and all that region who were two years old or under, according to the time which he had ascertained from the wise men. 17 Then was fulfilled what was spoken by the prophet Jeremiah

18 "A voice was heard in Ramah,
  wailing and loud lamentation,
  Rachel weeping for her children;
  she refused to be consoled,
  because they were no more.

Return from Egypt

Matthew 2. 19 – 23   (RSV)

19   But when Herod died, behold, an angel of the Lord appeared in a dream to Joseph in Egypt, saying 20   "Rise, take the child and his mother, and go to the land of Israel, for those who sought the child's life are dead".   21   And he rose and took the child and his mother, and went to the land of Israel.   22 But when he heard Archelaus reigned over Judaea in place of his father Herod, he was afraid to go there, and being warned in a dream he withdrew to the district of Galilee.   23   And he went and dwelt in a city called Nazareth, that what was spoken by the prophets might be fulfilled, "He shall be called a Nazarene".

Jesus as a boy in the Temple

Luke 2. 40 – 52   (RSV)

40   And the child grew and became strong, filled with wisdom; and the favour of God was upon him.

41   Now his parents went to Jerusalem every year at the feast of the Passover.   42 And when he was twelve years old, they went up according to custom; 43   and when the feast was ended as they were

returning, the boy Jesus stayed behind in Jerusalem. His parents did not know it 44 but supposing him to be in the company they went a day's journey, and they sought him among their kinsfolk and acquaintances; 45 and when they did not find him they returned to Jerusalem, seeking him. 46 After three days they found him in the temple, sitting among the teachers, listening to them, and asking them questions; 47 and all who heard him were amazed at his understanding and his answers. 48 And when they saw him they were astonished; and his mother said to him "Son, why have you treated us so? Behold, your father and I have been looking for you anxiously." 49 And he said to them "How is it that you sought me? Did you not know that I must be in my Father's house?" 50 And they did not understand the saying which he spoke to them. 51 And he went down with them and came to Nazareth, and was obedient to them; and his mother kept all these things in her heart.

52 And Jesus increased in wisdom and in stature, and in favour with God and man.

I find this a fascinating little story, mostly, I think, because it has such an unmistakeable ring of someone's special recollection, 'And his mother kept all these things in her heart'.

You can imagine years later, when finally the need had been recognised to gather and write down all the accounts while actual witnesses were still living, Mary, then probably an old lady, finally unlocking for the interviewer all the treasures she had kept and pondered in her heart.

She and Joseph travelling back from Jerusalem assuming Jesus to be with someone else in the long train of fellow travellers journeying back together, only to find a day later that he was not present. Their anxiety as they turned back to Jerusalem checking everywhere on the way; their astonishment when they finally find him in the temple calmly sitting discussing religious matters like an equal with the temple elders.

Their reproof to him. "How could you do this to us? Do you realise how worried we've been?" Only for him to respond with the totally baffling "Did you not realise that I had to be in my Father's house and about my Father's business?" But for him then to make it up to them by extra dutiful and mindful behaviour to them over the time that followed. Material indeed to be kept locked away in a mother's heart.

Chapter III
John and baptism

Matthew 3. 1 – 17 (RSV)

In those days came John the Baptist, preaching in the wilderness of Judea, 2 "Repent for the kingdom of heaven is at hand." 3 For this is he who was spoken of by the prophet Isaiah when he said

"The voice of one crying in the wilderness

Prepare the way of the Lord,

make his paths straight."

4 Now John wore a garment of Camel's hair, and a leather girdle around his waist; and his food was locusts and wild honey. 5 Then went out to him Jerusalem and all Judea and all the region about the Jordan, 6 and they were baptised by him in the river Jordan, confessing their sins.

7 But when he saw many of the Pharisees and Sadducees coming to baptism he said to them, "You brood of vipers! Who warned you to flee from the wrath to come? 8 Bear fruit that befits repentance, 9 and do not presume to say to yourselves, 'We have Abraham as our father;' for I tell you, God is able from these stones to raise up children to Abraham. 10 Even now the axe is laid to the root of the trees; every tree therefore that does not bear

good fruit is cut down and thrown into the fire.

11 "I baptise you with water for repentance, but he who is coming after me is mightier than I, whose sandals I am not worthy to carry; he will baptise you with the Holy Spirit and with fire. 12 His winnowing fork is in his hand and he will clear his threshing floor and gather his wheat into the granary, but the chaff he will burn with unquenchable fire.

13 Then Jesus came from Galilee to the Jordan to John, to be baptised by him. 14 John would have prevented him saying "I need to be baptised by you, and do you come to me?" 15 But Jesus answered him, "Let it be so now; for thus it is fitting for us to fulfil all righteousness." Then he consented. 16 And when Jesus was baptised, he went up immediately from the water, and behold the heavens were opened and he saw the spirit of God descending like a dove, and alighting on him; and lo, a voice from heaven saying "This is my beloved Son, with whom I am well pleased."

Matthew's version of this story differs from that given in the other three gospels in its quote given of John saying he was unworthy to 'carry' Jesus' sandals opposed to the, much loved by me, reference in the other three to his being unworthy to 'untie the thong' or 'lift the latch' of them.

But otherwise they are remarkably the same, reflecting the prominence and importance attached to this story in the Christian community.

Jesus' temptations in the wilderness

Matthew 4. 1 – 22 (RSV)

Then Jesus was led up by the spirit into the wilderness to be tempted by the devil. 2 And he fasted 40 days and 40 nights and afterwards he was hungry. 3 And the tempter came and said to him, "If you are the son of God, command these stones to become loaves of bread." 4 But he answered, "It is written 'Man shall not live by bread alone, but by every word that proceeds from the mouth of God.' "

5 Then the devil took him to the holy city, and set him on the pinnacle of the temple, 6 and said to him, "If you are the son of God, throw yourself down; for it is written

'He will give his angels charge of you' and

'On their hands they will bear you up lest you strike your foot against a stone.' "

7 Jesus said to him "Again it is written 'You shall not tempt the Lord your God.' " 8 Again, the devil took him to a very high mountain, and showed him all the kingdoms of the world and the glory of them:

9 and he said to him, "All these I will give you if you fall down and worship me." 10 Then Jesus said

to him "Begone, Satan! For it is written,

   'You shall worship the Lord your God

   and him only shall you serve.' "

11   Then the devil left him, and behold, angels came and ministered to him.

Again, it's a beautiful idea, Jesus needing and receiving angels ministering to him after his struggles with worldly temptations.

Arrest of John

Luke 3. 19 – 20   (RSV)

19   But Herod the tetrarch, who had been reproved by (John) for Herodias, his brother's wife, and for all the evil things that Herod had done, 20   added this to them all that he shut up John in prison.

Jesus starts to gather his disciples

Mark 1. 14 – 20   (RSV)

14   Now after John was arrested, Jesus came into Galilee, preaching the gospel of God,   15   and saying,   "The time is fulfilled, and the kingdom of God is at hand; repent and believe in the gospel".

   16   And passing along the Sea of Galilee, he saw

Simon and Andrew the brother of Simon casting a net in the sea; for they were fishermen. 17 And Jesus said to them "Follow me and I will make you become fishers of men." 18 And immediately they left their nets and followed him. 19 And going on a little farther, he saw James the son of Zebedee and John his brother, who were in their boat mending the nets. And immediately he called them; and they left their father Zebedee in the boat with the hired servants, and followed him.

One can't help feeling some sympathy for the parents and families of the new disciples, apparently simply abandoned by the sons they have nurtured, counted on, and trained in a trade that will assure them of a living. There is no reference to them complaining, but, whatever they thought of Jesus, they must surely have had equivocal feelings as they watched their boys walk away from the family business?

Wedding at Cana

John 2. 1 – 11 (RSV)
On the third day there was a marriage at Cana in Galilee and the mother of Jesus was there;

2 Jesus also was invited to the marriage, with his disciples. 3 When the wine gave out the mother of Jesus said to him "They have no wine". And Jesus

said to her "O woman, what have you to do with me? My hour has not yet come." 5 His mother said to the servants, "Do whatever he tells you."

6 Now six stone jars were standing there, for the Jewish rites of purification, each holding 20 or 30 gallons. 7 Jesus said to them "Fill the jars with water." And they filled them up to the brim. He said to them, "Now draw some out, and take it to the steward of the feast." So they took it. When the steward of the feast tasted the water now become wine, and did not know where it came from (though the servants who had drawn the water knew), the steward of the feast called the bridegroom 10 and said to him, "Every man serves the good wine first; and when men have drunk freely, then the poor wine; but you have kept the good wine until now." 11 This, the first of his signs, Jesus did at Cana in Galilee, and manifested his glory; and his disciples believed in him.

I have already stated my position on miracles. This one slightly stands on its own, though, in that almost all the others involve healing. This is simply a wonder on its own. The story only appears in John's Gospel, perhaps because the story was not widely known; perhaps because the others were a bit chary of it? I think of Jesus' mother, again, as a likely source for it, since it includes description of a private conversation between her and Jesus.

John may have liked it because he saw teaching opportunities in it. The features of the story could be used as symbols of an inner meaning comparing Christ's teaching with the old doctrines – the stone jars' water of the old Jewish purification rites turned to fine wine by Christ.

It is hard to get your head around the idea of water just becoming wine. In one way, though, the miracle is like all the others. It is about love. Mary sees the frightful impending shame and pain of the bridal family if they run out of wine in the middle of the feast. She knows there is an unstoppable power in Jesus, and she simply, ruthlessly, turns to him with the problem. Jesus gives her something like a rebuke. "My ministry has not yet started" and perhaps also "This is not really what my ministry is about."

But he cannot ever turn away from any call for his help. And so the miracle follows. What took place? It is fascinating to speculate, but something extraordinary happened. And so the story comes down to us.

Chapter IV
Jesus starts his ministry

Matthew 4. 23 - 7. 28   (RSV)

23   And he went about all Galilee, teaching in their synagogues and preaching the gospel of the kingdom and healing every disease and every infirmity among the people.   24   So his fame spread throughout all Syria, and they brought him all the sick, those afflicted with various diseases and pains, demoniacs, epileptics, and paralytics, and he healed them.   25   And great crowds followed him from Galilee and the Decapolis and Jerusalem and Judea and from beyond the Jordan.

Blessed...

5.   Seeing the crowds, he went up on the mountain, and when he sat down his disciples came to him.   2 And he opened his mouth and taught them, saying:

3   "Blessed are the poor in spirit, for theirs is the kingdom of heaven.

4   "Blessed are those who mourn, for they shall be comforted.

5   "Blessed are the meek for they shall inherit the

earth.

6 "Blessed are those who hunger and thirst for righteousness for they shall be satisfied.

7 "Blessed are the merciful, for they shall obtain mercy.

8 "Blessed are the peacemakers, for they shall be called sons of God.

10 "Blessed are those who are persecuted for righteousness sake, for theirs is the kingdom of heaven.

11 "Blessed are you when men revile you and persecute you and utter all kinds of evil against you falsely on my account. 12 Rejoice and be glad, for your reward is great in heaven, for so men persecuted the prophets who were before you.

13 "You are the salt of the earth; but if salt has lost its taste how shall its saltness be restored? It is no longer good for anything except to be thrown out and trodden underfoot by men.

Light of the world

14 "You are the light of the world. A city set on a hill cannot be hid. 15 Nor do men light a lamp and put it under a bushel, but on a stand, and it gives light to all in the house. 16 Let your light so shine before men, that they may see your good works and give glory to your Father who is in heaven.

17 "Think not that I have come to abolish the law and the prophets; I have come not to abolish but to fulfil them 18 For truly, I say to you, till heaven and earth pass away, not an iota, not a dot, will pass from the law until all is accomplished. 19 Whoever then relaxes one of the least of these commandments and teaches men so, shall be called least in the kingdom of heaven; but he who does them and teaches them shall be called great in the kingdom of heaven. 20 For I tell you unless your righteousness exceeds that of the scribes and Pharisees, you will never enter the kingdom of heaven.

21 "You have heard that it was said to the men of old, 'You shall not kill; and whoever kills shall be liable to judgement.' 22 But I say to you that everyone who is angry with his brother shall be liable to judgement; whoever insults his brother shall be liable to the council, and whoever says 'You fool!' shall be liable to the hell of fire. 3 So if you are offering your gift at the altar, and there remember that your brother has something against you, 24 leave your gift there before the altar and go: first be reconciled to your brother, and then come and offer your gift. 25 Make friends quickly with your accuser, while you are going with him to court, lest your accuser hand you over to the judge, and the judge to the guard, and you be put in prison; 26 Truly, I say to you, you will never get out till you have paid the

last penny.

27 "You have heard that it was said 'You shall not commit adultery', 28 But I say to you that everyone who looks at a woman lustfully has already committed adultery with her in his heart. 29 If your right eye causes you to sin, pluck it out and throw it away; it is better that you lose one of your members than that your whole body be thrown into hell. 30 And if your right hand causes you to sin, cut it off and throw it away; it is better that you lose one of your members than that your whole body go into hell.

31 It was also said, 'Whoever divorces his wife, let him give her a certificate of divorce.' 32 But I say to you that everyone who divorces his wife, except on the ground of unchastity, makes her an adulteress; and whoever marries a divorced woman commits adultery.

33 "Again you have heard that it was said to the men of old, 'You shall not swear falsely, but shall perform to the Lord what you have sworn.' 34 But I say to you, Do not swear at all, either by heaven, for it is the throne of God, 35 or by the earth, for it is his footstool, or by Jerusalem, which is the city of the great King. 36 And do not swear by your head, for you cannot make one hair white or black. 37 Let what you say be simply 'Yes' or 'No'; anything more than this comes from evil.

38 You have heard that it was said, 'An eye for

an eye and a tooth for a tooth.' 39 But I say to you, Do not resist one who is evil. But if anyone strikes you on the right cheek, turn to him the other also; 40 and if anyone would sue you and take your coat, let him have your cloak as well; 41 and if anyone forces you to go one mile, go with him two miles. 42 Give to him who begs from you, and do not refuse him who would borrow from you.

43 "You have heard that it was said,'You shall love your neighbour and hate your enemy.' 44 But I say to you, Love your enemies and pray for those who persecute you, 45 so that you may be sons of your Father who is in heaven; for he makes his sun rise on the evil and on the good, and sends rain on the just and on the unjust. 46 For if you love those who love you, what reward have you? Do not even the tax collectors do the same? 47 And if you salute only your brethren, what more are you doing than others? Do not even the Gentiles do the same? 48 You therefore, must be perfect, as your heavenly Father is perfect.

Praying

6. "Beware of practising your piety before men in order to be seen by them; for then you will have no reward from your Father who is in heaven.

2 "Thus, when you give alms, sound no trumpet

before you, as the hypocrites do in the synagogues and in the streets, that they may be praised by men. Truly, I say to you they have received their reward. 3 But when you give alms, do not let your left hand know what your right hand is doing, 4 so that your alms may be in secret; and your Father who sees in secret will reward you.

5 "And when you pray you must not be like the hypocrites; for they love to stand and pray in the synagogues and at the street corners, that they may be seen by men. Truly, I say to you they have received their reward. 6 But when you pray, go into your room and shut the door and pray to your Father who is in secret; and your Father who sees in secret will reward you.

7 "And in praying do not heap up empty phrases as the Gentiles do; for they think they will be heard for their many words. 8 Do not be like them, for your Father knows what you need before you ask him.

9 Pray then like this

Our Father who art in heaven,

Hallowed be thy name,

10 Thy kingdom come

Thy will be done,

On earth as it is in heaven.

11 Give us this day our daily bread;

12 And forgive us our debts,

As we also have forgiven our debtors;

13 And lead us not into temptation
But deliver us from evil.

14 For if you forgive men their trespasses, your heavenly Father also will forgive you; 15 but if you do not forgive men their trespasses, neither will your Father forgive your trespasses.

16 "And when you fast, do not look dismal, like the hypocrites, for they disfigure their faces that their fasting may be seen by men. Truly, I say to you, they have received their reward 17 But when you fast, anoint your head and wash your face, 18 that your fasting may not be seen by men but by your father who is in secret; and your Father who sees in secret will reward you.

19 Do not lay up for yourselves treasures on earth, where moth and rust consume and where thieves break in and steal, but lay up for yourselves treasure in heaven, where neither moth nor rust consumes and where thieves do not break in and steal. 21 For where your treasure is, there will your heart be also.

Do not be anxious

22 "The eye is the lamp of the body. So, if your eye is sound, your whole body will be full of light; 23 but if your eye is not sound, your whole body will be full of darkness. If then the light in you is darkness,

how great is that darkness!

24 "No one can serve two masters; for either he will hate the one and love the other, or he will be devoted to the one and despise the other. You cannot serve God and mammon.

25 "Therefore I tell you, do not be anxious about your life, what you shall eat or what you shall drink nor about your body, what you shall put on. Is not life more than food, and the body more than clothing? 26 Look at the birds of the air: they neither sow nor reap nor gather into barns, and yet your heavenly Father feeds them. Are you not of more value than they? 27 And which of you by being anxious can add one cubit to his span of life? 28 And why are you anxious about clothing? Consider the lilies of the field, how they grow; they neither toil nor spin, 9 yet I tell you, even Solomon in all his glory was not arrayed like one of these. 30 But if God so clothes the grass of the field, which today is alive and tomorrow is thrown into the oven, will he not much more clothe you, O men of little faith? 31 'Therefore do not be anxious, saying ''What shall we eat?' or 'What shall we wear?' 32 For the Gentiles seek all these things; and your heavenly Father knows that you need them all. 33 But seek first his kingdom and his righteousness, and all these things shall be yours as well.

34 "Therefore do not be anxious about tomorrow, for tomorrow will be anxious for itself. Let the day' s

own trouble be sufficient for the day.

Judge not

7. "Judge not that you be not judged. 2 For with the judgement you pronounce you will be judged, and the measure you give will be the measure you get. 3 Why do you see the speck in your brother's eye, but do not notice the log that is in your own eye? Or how can you say to your brother, 'Let me take the speck out of your eye,' when there is a log in your own eye? You hypocrite, first take the log out of your own eye, and then you will see clearly to take the speck out of your brother's eye.

6 "Do not give dogs what is holy; and do not throw your pearls before swine, lest they trample them underfoot and turn to attack you.

7 "Ask and it will be given to you; seek, and you will find; knock, and it will be opened to you. 8 For everyone who asks receives, and he who seeks finds, and to him who knocks it will be opened. 9 Or what man of you, if his son asks him for bread, will give him a stone? 10 Or if he asks for a fish will give him a serpent? 11 If you then, who are evil, know how to give good gifts to your children, how much more will your Father who is in heaven give good things to those who ask him? 12 So whatever you wish that men would do to you, do so to them:

for this is the law and the prophets.

13 "Enter by the narrow gate; for the gate is wide and the way is easy, that leads to destruction, and those who enter by it are many. 14 For the gate is narrow and the way is hard, that leads to life, and those who find it are few.

15 "Beware of false prophets, who come to you in sheep's clothing, but inwardly are ravenous wolves. 16 You will know them by their fruits. Are grapes gathered from thorns, or figs from thistles? 17 So, every sound tree bears good fruit, but the bad tree bears evil fruit. 18 A sound tree cannot bear evil fruit, nor can a bad tree bear good fruit. 19 Every tree that does not bear good fruit is cut down and thrown into the fire. 20 Thus you will know them by their fruits.

21 "Not everyone who says to me 'Lord, Lord' shall enter the kingdom of heaven, but he who does the will of my Father who is in heaven. 22 On that day many will say to me, 'Lord, Lord, did we not prophesy in your name, and cast out demons in your name, and do many mighty works in your name'?

23 And then I will declare to them ' 'I never knew you; depart from me evildoers.'

24 "Everyone then who hears these words of mine and does them will be like a wise man who built his house upon the rock; 25 and the rain fell, and the floods came, and the winds blew and beat upon that house but it did not fall, because it had been

founded on the rock. 26 and everyone who hears these words of mine and does not do them will be like a foolish man who built his house upon the sand; 27 and the rain fell, and the floods came, and the winds blew and beat against that house and it fell: and great was the fall of it."

28 And when Jesus finished these sayings, the crowds were astonished at his teaching 29 for he taught them as one who had authority, and not as their scribes.

I used, as a boy, to be somewhat dissatisfied with the Lord's prayer. It did not, I felt, give the guarantee of safety that I was looking for. The 'evil' in 'Deliver us from evil' has an ambivalence about it, not like the precision I would have hoped for, as, for example, 'harm', or 'bad things'. It was only later that I began to accept that the prayer was not intended as a personal insurance policy.

It was instead a plea to God to help us to stay on the path to our true selves, and so to God. To serve this purpose it is perfect. It begins with acknowledgement of God; then statement of the desire for his purposes to be fulfilled; acceptance, sometimes perhaps with apprehension, that his will should also be ours; then the generous allowance for us to pray simply that we all may have food each day, delivery of which may, at times, be dependent on the actions of ourselves and others, the 'Bread' also referring perhaps to the gift of the word of God: the acknowledgement of the ways in which we may have failed in the pursuit of God's purpose, with a reminder to ourselves to behave to those who have failed us with the same unreserved love we can count on from God; finally, the plea to God to help us to stay free from acts that are the opposite of doing God's will, that stain and compromise ourselves and harm ourselves and others.

I think I prefer the use of the word 'debts' as opposed to 'sins' in 'forgive us our debts'. It describes better for me the whole range of ways in which I may have fallen down over the past period – ways in which I have not lived up to how I know I should have lived, things I have failed to do as well as things I have done which I wish I had'nt. 'Sins' seems to me much more prescriptive of actual shameful acts, and I find I can sometimes get quite annoyed to be always invited in a service to confess my 'sins' when I actually may have had a week in which I reckon I have'nt done too badly! As if, to be a Christian, you have constantly to be bemoaning and flagellating yourself for your inadequacies.

Chapter V
Jesus healing

Matthew 8. 1 – 17 (RSV)

8.   When he came down from the mountain, great crowds followed him; 2 and behold, a leper came to him and knelt before him, saying, "Lord, if you will you can make me clean."   3 And he stretched out his hand and touched him saying, "I will; be clean." And immediately his leprosy was cleansed. 4 And Jesus said to him,"See that you say nothing to anyone; but go, show yourself to the priest, and offer the gift that Moses commanded, for a proof to the people."

   5 As he entered Capernaum a centurion came forward to him, beseeching him 6 and saying, "Lord my servant is lying paralysed at home, in terrible distress."   7   and he said to him, "I will come and heal him." 8   But the centurion answered him, "Lord I am not worthy to have you come under my roof; but only say the word, and my servant will be healed. 9 For I am a man under authority, with soldiers under me; and I say to one, 'Go' and he goes, and to another 'Come', and he comes, and to my slave, 'Do this," and he does it." 10 When Jesus heard him,

65

he marvelled, and said to those who followed him, "Truly, I say to you, not even in Israel have I found such faith. 11 I tell you, many will come from East and West and sit at table with Abraham, Isaac, and Jacob in the kingdom of heaven, 12 while the sons of the kingdom will be thrown into the outer darkness; there men will weep and gnash their teeth." 13 And to the centurion Jesus said, "Go; be it done for you as you have believed." And the servant was healed at that very moment.

14 And when Jesus entered Peter's house, he saw his mother-in-law lying sick with a fever; 15 he touched her hand, and the fever left her, and she rose and served him . 16 That evening they brought to him many who were possessed with Demons; and he cast out the spirits with a word, and healed all who were sick. 17 This was to fulfil what was spoken by the prophet Isaiah: "He took our infirmities and bore our diseases.".

The paralysed man

Luke 5. 17 – 26 (RSV)

17 On one of those days, as he was teaching, there were Pharisees and teachers of the law sitting by, who had come from every village of Galilee and Judea and Jerusalem; and the power of the Lord was with him to heal. 18 And behold, men were

bringing on a bed a man who was paralysed, and they sought to bring him in and lay him before Jesus; 19 but finding no way to bring him in, because of the crowd, they went up on the roof and let him down with his bed through the tiles into the midst before Jesus. 20 And when he saw their faith he said, "Man, your sins are forgiven you." 21 And the scribes and Pharisees began to question, saying 'Who is this that speaks blasphemies? Who can forgive sins but God only?" 22 When Jesus perceived their questionings, he answered them, "Why do you question in your hearts? 23 Which is easier to say, 'Your sins are forgiven you', or to say, 'Rise and walk'? 24 But that you may know that the Son of man has authority on earth to forgive sin "' - he said to the man who was paralysed – "I say to you, rise, take your bed and go home." 25 And immediately he rose before them, and took up that on which he lay, and went home, glorifying God. 26 And amazement seized them all, and they glorified God and were filled with awe, saying, "We have seen strange things today."

I think this is such a poignant image. The men so desperate to get their friend or relation to Jesus that they climb onto the roof with him, take the tiles away and let him down on his bed right in front of Jesus. Jesus, moved by their faith, immediately acts, and responding to the generally held belief that disabilities were a punishment for past sins, simply says: "'Your sins are forgiven".

When he sees the scribes and Pharisees muttering "Who does he think he is to presume he can forgive sins?" he says: "What is the problem? Does it make any difference if I say 'Your sins are forgiven' or 'Rise up and walk'? But in fact forgiveness is integral to God's love, and to show you that as such I have absolute authority to make it available to all who truly seek it, I say to the paralysed man 'Rise, take up your bed and go home'."

And amazement seized them all.

Levi and the tax collectors

Luke 5. 27 – 39   (RSV)

27   After this he went out and saw a tax collector, named Levi, sitting at the tax office; and he said to him, "Follow me."   28   And he left everything, and rose and followed him.

29 And Levi made him a great feast in his house; and there was a large company of tax collectors and others sitting at table with them.   30   And the Pharisees and the scribes murmured against his disciples, saying, "Why do you eat and drink with tax collectors and sinners?"

31   And Jesus answered them, "Those who are well have no need of a physician, but those who are

sick; 32 I have not come to call the righteous, but sinners to repentance."

33 And they said to him, "The disciples of John fast often and offer prayers and so do the disciples of the Pharisees, but yours eat and drink". 34 And Jesus said to them, "Can you make wedding guests fast while the bridegroom is with them? 35 The days will come when the bridegroom is taken away from them, and then they will fast in those days." 36 He told them a parable also: "No one tears a piece from a new garment and puts it upon an old garment; if he does, he will tear the new, and the piece from the new will not match the old. 37 And no one puts new wine into old wineskins; if he does the new wine will burst the skins and it will be spilled, and the skins will be destroyed. 38 But new wine must be put into fresh wineskins. 39 And no one after drinking old wine desires new; for he says, 'The old is good.' "

I've always had the feeling that Jesus enjoyed himself at these tax collector gatherings, while acknowledging, yes indeed, that they were the right constituency for his attention; although perhaps it could be said that the scribes and Pharisees were in the same category of need?

Certainly one feels a publicans and sinners get together was likely to be considerably more convivial than an equivalent scribes and Pharisees assembly.

Despised and hated by most of the community for their widespread abuse of power and extortionate tax demands, the Levis of the world responded with instinctive warmth to Jesus' open acceptance of them in human terms. It always seems there was an enthusiastic attendance at functions where he was present; and, one senses, a readiness to hear what he has to say. So, indeed, a happy coincidence between the evangelical and the recreational!

Dinner with a Pharisee. Woman wiping Jesus' feet with her hair

Luke 7. 36 – 50   (RSV)

36 One of the Pharisees asked him to eat with him, and he went into the Pharisees house, and took his place at table. 37 And behold, a woman of the city, who was a sinner, when she learned that he was at table in the Pharisees house, brought an alabaster flask of ointment, 38 and standing behind him at his feet, weeping, she began to wet his feet with her tears, and wiped them with the hair of her head, and kissed his feet, and anointed them with the ointment. 39 Now when the Pharisee who had invited him saw

it, he said to himself, "If this man were a prophet, he would have known who and what sort of woman this is who is touching him, for she is a sinner." 40 And Jesus answering said to him, "Simon, I have something to say to you." And he answered, "What is it, Teacher?" 41 "A certain creditor had two debtors; one owed five hundred denarii, and the other fifty. 42 When they could not pay, he forgave them both. Now which of them will love him more?" 43 Simon answered, "The one, I suppose, to whom he forgave more." And he said to him, "You have judged rightly." 44 Then turning toward the woman he said to Simon, "Do you see this woman? I entered your house, you gave me no water for my feet, but she has wet my feet with her tears and wiped them with her hair. 45 You gave me no kiss, but from the time I came in she has not ceased to kiss my feet. 46 You did not anoint my head with oil, but she has anointed my feet with ointment. 47 Therefore, I tell you, her sins, which are many, are forgiven, for she loved much; but he who is forgiven little, loves little." 48 And he said to her, "Your sins are forgiven." 49 Then those who were at table with him began to say among themselves, "Who is this, who even forgives sins?" 50 And he said to the woman, "Your faith has saved you; go in peace."

The 'woman of the city' is Mary, sister of Martha and Lazarus, as identified later in John chapter 11. Is she also Mary Magdalene as referred to in Luke chapter 8 in the next paragraph?

Going with apostles and women who provided for them

Luke 8. 1 – 3   (RSV)
Soon afterward he went on through cities and villages, preaching and bringing the good news of the kingdom of God. And the twelve were with him, 2 and also some women who had been healed of evil spirits and infirmities: Mary, called Magdalene, from whom seven demons had gone out, 3   and Joanna, the wife of Chuza, Herod's steward, and Susanna, and many others, who provided for them out of their means.

This is one of the few references I know to the women disciples of Jesus; Mary Magdalene, Joanna, Susanna, 'and many others'; and the only reference I know to the importance of the part played by them, 'who provided for them out of their means'.

Divine mission or not, but food, shelter, clothing would have to be found on a daily basis, and these women were the means by which God responded to the trust placed in Him to 'give this day the daily bread' that allowed Jesus to concentrate exclusively on God's work in his ministry.

Foxes have holes

Luke 9. 57 – 62   (RSV)

57 As they were going along the road, a man said to him, "I will follow you wherever you go." 58   And Jesus said to him, "Foxes have holes, and birds of the air have nests; but the Son of man has nowhere to lay his head." 59   To another he said , "Follow me." But he said , "Lord, let me first go and bury my father." 60   But he said to him, "Leave the dead to bury their own dead; but as for you go and proclaim the kingdom of God." 61   Another said, "I will follow you, Lord; but let me first say farewell to those at my home. 62   Jesus said to him, "No one who puts his hand to the plough and looks back is fit for the kingdom of God."

I always think this sounds such a bleak, chillingly uncompromising response, but Jesus, I think, is just making sure that the commitment in question is understood. It demands heart and soul and perhaps body. Come to him when you are ready.

Parable of the good Samaritan

Luke 10. 25 – 37 (RSV)
25 And behold, a lawyer stood up to put him to the

test, saying, "Teacher, what shall I do to inherit eternal life?" 26 He said to him, "What is written in the law? How do you read?" 27 And he answered, "You shall love the Lord your God with all your heart, and with all your soul, and with all your strength, and with all your mind; and your neighbour as yourself." 28 And he said to him, "You have answered right; do this, and you will live."

29   But he, desiring to justify himself, said to Jesus,"And who is my neighbour?" 30   Jesus replied, "A man was going down from Jerusalem to Jericho, and he fell among robbers, who stripped him and beat him, and departed, leaving him half dead. 31 Now by chance a priest was going down that road; and when he saw him passed by on the other side. 32 So likewise a Levite, when he came to the place and saw him, passed by on the other side. 33 But a Samaritan, as he journeyed, came to where he was; and when he saw him, he had compassion, 34 and went to him and bound up his wounds, pouring on oil and wine; then set him on his own beast and brought him to an inn, and took care of him.

35 And the next day he took out two denarii and gave them to the innkeeper, saying, "Take care of him; and what ever more you spend, I will repay you when I come back. 36 Which of these three, do you think, proved neighbour to the man who fell among the robbers?" 37   He said "The one who showed

mercy on him." And Jesus said to him, "Go and do likewise."

Martha and Mary

Luke 10. 38 – 41 (RSV)

38   Now as they went on their way, he entered a village; and a woman named Martha received him into her house.   39   And she had a sister called Mary, who sat at the Lord's feet and listened to his teaching.   40   But Martha was distracted with much serving; and she went to him and said "Lord, do you not care that my sister has left me to serve alone? Tell her then to help me."   41   But the Lord answered her, "Martha, Martha, you are anxious and troubled about many things: 42   one thing is needful. Mary has chosen the good portion, which shall not be taken away from her."

Mary, the 'woman of the city' referred to earlier in Luke chapter 7 who wet Jesus' feet with her tears and wiped them with her hair at the Pharisee's house where he was having dinner. The question is whether she is also Mary Magdalene.

Chapter VI

He casts out demons by the prince of demons

Mark 3. 19 – 30   (RSV)

19 Then he went home; 20 and the crowd came together again, so that they could not even eat. 21 And when his family heard it they went out to seize him, for people were saying, "He is beside himself." 22 And the scribes who came down from Jerusalem said, "He is possessed by Beelzebub, and by the prince of demons he casts out the demons". 23 And he called them to him, and said to them in parables,"How can Satan cast out Satan? 24 If a kingdom is divided against itself that kingdom cannot stand. 25 And if a house is divided against itself, that house will not be able to stand. 26 And if Satan has risen up against himself and is divided, he cannot stand but is coming to an end. 27 But no one can enter a strong man's house and plunder his goods, unless he first binds the strong man; then indeed he may plunder his house. 28 "Truly I say to you all sins will be forgiven the sons of men, and whatever blasphemies they offer; 29 but whoever blasphemes against the Holy Spirit never has forgiveness but is guilty of an eternal sin" - 30   for

they had said, "He has an unclean spirit."

As a boy I used to be so scared by that statement. What if I had inadvertently committed the sin against the Holy Spirit? I think we have to take account of Jesus the man here. What anger he must have felt at the attempt to portray the ultimate holiness of healing mind and body as the works of the devil.

Wickedness worthy indeed of reference to eternal sin. And, of course, while they persisted in their upside down world, eternal sin was, in a sense, what they were seeking. I remember, too, though, the all embracing love and welcome of the Prodigal Son and the seventy times seven.

Jesus the man was explored further in Martin Scorsese's *The Last Temptation of Christ*, a film I resisted going to see, convinced from what I had heard that I would find it objectionable. I was persuaded in the end by an atheistic or agnostic friend.

Christ is on the cross with the vision of his life unreeling before his eyes.

At some point Jesus must surely have looked with envy at ordinary people, simply living ordinary lives, free to find fulfilment in relationships with other people, having children. Would he not have liked to experience that fulfilment? Can we doubt that there was someone with whom Jesus would willingly have settled down and shared his life, and there must have sometime been a yearning to experience that joy.

That unfulfilled desire now returns to him, intensified by the persistent image of a beautiful child who might have been the fruit of such a union. Eventually Jesus yields to the temptation to wish he had chosen that course.

Instantly his life is reversed. There is no cross. He has lived a life of domestic bliss with a lovely partner (Mary Magdalene?) and the crowning blessing of the beautiful child he had imagined. Instinctively Jesus knows something is wrong. He challenges the image, and at once the child's face dissolves into that of the devil, luring him from his path. The countdown to irrevocability has begun. Desperately Jesus drags himself on his elbows back to the cross and his destiny.

His mother and brothers

Mark 3. 31 – 35 (RSV)

31 And his mother and his brothers came; and standing outside they sent to him and called him. 32 And a crowd was sitting about him; and they said to him,"Your mother and your brothers are outside, asking for you 33 And he replied, "Who are my mother and my brothers?" 34 And looking around on those who sat about him, he said, "Here are my

mother and my brothers! 35 Whoever does the will
of God is my brother, and sister, and mother."

Again, I always think Jesus' response to being told
his mother and his family were outside is so hurtful,
so needlessly unfeeling, but in a way it reflects the
hard elements of following his path. You can count
on infinite love, but not necessarily cosiness.

Parable of the sower

Matthew 13. 1 – 23   (RSV)
That same day Jesus went out of the house and sat
beside the sea. 2 And great crowds gathered about
him, so that he got into a boat and sat there; and the
whole crowd stood on the beach. 3   And he told
them many things in parables, saying: " A sower
went out to sow. 4 And as he sowed, some seeds
fell along the path, and the birds came and devoured
them. 5   Other seeds fell on rocky ground, where
they had not much soil, and immediately they sprang
up, since they had no depth of soil, 6 but when the
sun rose they were scorched: and since they had no
root, they withered away. 7   Other seeds fell upon
thorns, and the thorns grew up and choked them. 8
Other seeds fell on good soil and brought forth grain,
some a hundredfold, some sixty, some thirty. 9 He

who has ears let him hear.

10   Then the disciples came and said to him, "Why do you speak to them in parables?" 11 And he answered them "To you it has been given to know the secrets of the kingdom of heaven, but to them it has not been given. 12 For to him who has will more be given, and he will have abundance; but from him who has not, even what he has will be taken away. 13 This is why I speak to them in parables, because seeing they do not see, and hearing they do not hear, nor do they understand. 14 With them indeed is fulfilled the prophecy of Isaiah -

You shall indeed hear but never understand
and you shall indeed see but never perceive
15 For this people's heart has grown dull,
and their ears are heavy of hearing
and their eyes they have closed,
lest they should perceive with their eyes,
and hear with their ears,
and understand with their heart,
and turn for me to heal them.

16 But blessed are your eyes, for they see, and your ears for they hear. 17 Truly, I say to you, many prophets and righteous men longed to see what you see, and did not see it, and to hear what you hear, and did not hear it.

18 "Hear then the parable of the sower. 19 When anyone hears the word of the kingdom and

does not understand it, the evil one comes and snatches away what is sown in his heart; this is what was sown along the path. 20 As for what was sown on rocky ground, this is he who hears the word and immediately receives it with joy; 21 yet he has no root in himself, but endures for a while, and when tribulation or persecution arises on account of the word, immediately he falls away. 22 As for what was sown among thorns, this is he who hears the word, but the cares of the world and the delight in riches chokes the word and it proves unfruitful. 23 As for what was sown on good soil, this is he who hears the word and understands it; he indeed bears fruit, and yields in one case a hundredfold in another sixty, and another thirty".

Jesus appears to have instinctively understood the, otherwise, hard lesson that performance-oriented teachers have to learn – that people only really master new knowledge and make it their own by discovering it for themselves in their own way, normally via a series of trial and error blunders. Jesus buries his message in a story, and leaves his listeners to puzzle it out. When they do, after probably a series of false starts, it will have become truly part of their own thinking.

Someone asking for loaves.
Someone asking for fish

Luke 11 5 – 13 (RSV)

5   And he said to them, "Which of you who has a friend will go to him at midnight and say to him, "Friend, lend me three loaves; 6 for a friend of mine has arrived on a journey, and I have nothing to set before him;   7   and he will answer from within, 'Do not bother me; the door is now shut, and my children are with me in bed; I cannot get up and give you anything'? 8 I tell you, though he will not get up and give him anything because he is his friend, yet because of his importunity he will rise and give him whatever he needs. 9 And I tell you, Ask, and it will be given you; seek, and you will find; knock, and it will be opened to you. 10 For every one who asks receives, and he who seeks finds, and to him who knocks it will be opened.   11   What father among you, if his son asks for a fish, will instead of a fish give him a serpent; 12 or if he asks for an egg, will give him a scorpion? 13 If you then, who are evil, know how to give good gifts to your children, how much more will the heavenly Father give the Holy Spirit to those who ask him! "

Rich towards God

Luke 12. 13 – 21 (RSV)

13 One of the multitude said to him, "Teacher, bid my brother divide the inheritance with me." 14 But he said to him, "Man, who made me a charge or the divider over you?" 15 And he said to them, "Take heed, and beware of all covetousness: for a man's life does not consist in the abundance of his possessions". 16 And he told them a parable, saying, "The land of a rich man brought forth plentifully; 17 and he thought to himself, 'What shall I do, for I have nowhere to store my crops?' 18 And he said, 'I will do this; I will pull down my barns, and build larger ones; and there I will store all my grain and my goods. 19 And I will say to my soul, Soul, you have ample goods laid up for many years; take your ease, eat, drink, be merry. .20 But God said to him, 'Fool! This night your soul is required of you; and the things you have prepared whose will they be?' 21 So is he who lays up treasure for himself, and is not rich toward God."

Lamp under a bushel. Grain of mustard seed

Mark 4. 24 – 34 (RSV)

24 And he said to them, "Take heed what you hear; the measure you give will be the measure you get, and still more will be given you. 25 For to him who has will more be given; and from him who has not, even what he has will be taken away."

26 And he said, "The kingdom of God is as if a man should scatter seed upon the ground, 27 and should sleep and rise night and day, and the seed should sprout and grow, he knows not how. 28 The earth produces of itself, first the blade, then the ear, then the full grain in the ear. 29 But when the grain is ripe, at once he puts in the sickle, because the harvest has come."

30 And he said, "with what can we compare the kingdom of God, or what parable shall we use for it? 31 It is like a grain of mustard seed, which, when sown upon the ground is the smallest of all the seeds on earth; 32 yet when it is sown it grows up and becomes the greatest of all shrubs, and puts forth large branches, so that the birds of the air can make nests in its shade.

Parable of the good seed, Kingdom of Heaven like leaven, a treasure, a net

Matthew 13. 24 – 30, 33 – 52 (RSV)

24 Another parable he put before them, saying,"The kingdom of heaven may be compared to a man who sowed good seed in his field;   25   but while men were sleeping, his enemy came and sowed weeds among the wheat, and went away. 26 So when the plants came up and bore grain, then the weeds appeared also.   27   And the servants of the householder came and said to him, 'Sir, did you not sow good seed in your field? How then has it weeds?' 28 He said to them, 'An enemy has done this.' The servants said to him, 'Then do you want us to go and gather them?' But he said,'No; lest in gathering the weeds you root up the wheat along with them. 30   Let both grow together until the harvest; and at harvest time I will tell the reapers, Gather the weeds first and bind them in bundles to be burned, but gather the wheat into my barn"'

33 He told them another parable, "The kingdom of heaven is like leaven which a woman took and hid in three measures of flour, till it was all leavened."

34 All this Jesus said to the crowds in parables; indeed he said nothing to them without a parable. 35   This was to fulfil what was spoken by the prophet; "I will open my mouth in parables, I will offer what has been hidden since the foundation of the world"

36   Then he left the crowds and went into the house. And his disciples came to him saying,

"Explain to us the parable of the weeds of the field."
37 He answered, "He who sows the good seed is the Son of man; 38 the field is the world, and the good seed means the sons of the kingdom; the weeds are the sons of the evil one, 39 and the enemy who sowed them is the devil; the harvest is the close of the age, and the reapers are angels. 40 Just as the weeds are gathered and burned with fire, so will it be at the close of the age. 41 The Son of man will send his angels, and they will gather out of his kingdom all causes of sin and all evildoers, 42 and throw them into the furnace of fire; there men will weep and gnash their teeth. 43 Then the righteous will shine like the sun in the kingdom of their Father. He who has ears let him hear.

44 The kingdom of heaven is like treasure hidden in a field which a man found and covered up; then in his joy he goes and sells all that he has and buys that field.

45 "Again, the kingdom of heaven is like a merchant in search of fine pearls, 46 who on finding one pearl of great value, went and sold all that he had and bought it.

47 "Again the kingdom of heaven is like a net which was thrown into the sea and gathered fish of every kind; 48 when it was full, men drew it ashore and sat down and sorted the good into vessels but threw away the bad 49 So it will be at the close of the age. The Angels will come out and separate the

evil from the righteous, 50 and throw them into the furnace of fire; there men will weep and gnash their teeth

51 "Have you understood all this? They said to him, "Yes."" 52 And he said to them, " Therefore every scribe who has been trained for the kingdom of heaven is like a householder who brings out of his treasure what is new and what is old."

Chapter VII
The boat in the storm

Mark 4. 35 – 41   (RSV)

35 On that day, when evening had come, he said to them, "Let us go across to the other side."

36   And leaving the crowd, they took him with them in the boat, just as he was. And other boats were with him. 37 And a great storm of wind arose, and the waves beat into the boat so that the boat was already filling. 38   But he was in the stern, asleep on the cushion; and they woke him and said to him, "Teacher, do you not care if we perish?" 39 And he awoke and rebuked the wind, and said to the sea, "Peace! Be still!" And the wind ceased, and there was a great calm. 40 He said to them, "Why are you afraid? Have you no faith?" 41 And they were filled with awe, and said to one another, "Who then is this, that even wind and sea obey him?"

I love this image of Jesus asleep on the cushion and his terrified disciples watching in increasing desperation and exasperation for him to wake up. How difficult it would be to put your trust and yourself entirely into God's hands to dispense in accordance with his will.

The Gadarene Swine

Luke 8. 26 – 39   (RSV)

26   Then they arrived at the country of the Gerasenes, which is opposite Galilee. 27 And as he stepped out on land there met him a man from the city who had demons; for a long time he had worn no clothes and he lived not in a house but among the tombs. 28 When he saw Jesus he cried out and fell down before him, and said with a loud voice, "What have you to do with me, Jesus, Son of the Most High God? I beseech you, do not torment me." 29 For he had commanded the unclean spirits to come out of the man. (For many a time it had seized him; he was kept under guard, and bound with chains and fetters, but he broke the bonds and was driven by the demon into the desert.) 30 Jesus then asked him, "What is your name?" And he said, "Legion"; for many demons had entered him.   31   And they begged him not to command them to depart into the abyss. 32 Now a large herd of swine was feeding there on the hillside; and they begged him to let them enter them. So he gave them leave. 33 Then the Demons came out of the man and entered the swine, and the herd rushed down the steep bank into the lake and were drowned.

34 When the herdsmen saw what had happened, they fled, and told it in the city and in the country. 35

89

Then people went out to see what had happened, and they came to Jesus, and found the man from whom the demons had gone, sitting at the feet of Jesus, clothed and in his right mind; and they were afraid. 36 And those who had seen it told them how he who had been possessed with demons was healed. 37 Then all the people of the surrounding country of the Gerasenes asked him to depart from them; for they were seized with great fear; so he got into the boat and returned. 38 The man from whom the Demons had gone begged that he might be with him; but he sent him away saying, 39 "Return to your home, and declare how much God has done for you." And he went away, proclaiming throughout the whole city how much Jesus had done for him.

Jairus' daughter, and the woman with the flow of blood

Mark 5. 21 – 43   (RSV)

21 And when Jesus had crossed again in the boat to the other side, a great crowd gathered about him; and he was beside the sea. 22 Then came one of the rulers of the synagogue, Jairus by name; and seeing him he fell at his feet, 23 and besought him, saying, "My little daughter is at the point of death. Come and lay your hands on her, so that she may

be made well, and live." 24 And he went with him. And a great crowd thronged about him. 25 And there was a woman who had had a flow of blood for twelve years, 26 and who had suffered much under many physicians, and had spent all that she had, and was no better but rather grew worse. 27 She had heard the reports about Jesus, and came up behind him in the crowd and touched his garment. 28 For she said, "If I touch even his garments, I shall be made well." 29 And immediately the haemorrhage ceased; and she felt in her body that she was healed of her disease. 30 And Jesus, perceiving in himself that power had gone forth from him, immediately turned about in the crowd, and said, "Who touched my garments?" 31 And his disciples said to him, "You see the crowd pressing around you, and yet you say, 'Who touched me?'" 32 And he looked around to see who had done it. 33 But the woman, knowing what had been done to her, came in fear and trembling and fell down before him, and told him the whole truth. 34 And he said to her, "Daughter your faith has made you well; go in peace, and be healed of your disease."

35 While he was still speaking, there came from the ruler's house some who said, "Your daughter is dead. Why trouble the Teacher any further?" 36 But ignoring what they said, Jesus said to the ruler of the synagogue, "Do not fear, only believe." 37 And he allowed no one to follow him except Peter and

James and John the brother of James. 38 When they came to the house of the ruler of the synagogue, he saw a tumult, and people weeping and wailing loudly. 39 And when he had entered he said to them, "Why do you make a tumult and weep? The child is not dead but sleeping." 40 And they laughed at him. But he put them all outside, and took the child's father and mother and those who were with him, and went in where the child was. 41 Taking her by the hand he said to her, "Talitha cumi;" which means, "Little girl, I say to you, arise." 42 And immediately the girl got up and walked (she was 12 years of age), and they were immediately overcome with amazement. 43 and he strictly charged them that no one should know this, and told them to give her something to eat.

I find these two stories amongst the most moving in the New Testament.

Nicodemus

John 3 1 – 15 (RSV)
Now there was a man of the Pharisees named Nicodemus, a ruler of the Jews. 2 This man came to Jesus by night and said to him, "Rabbi, we know that you are a teacher come from God; for no one

can do these signs that you do, unless God is with him." 3 Jesus answered him, "Truly, truly, I say to you, unless one is born anew, he cannot see the kingdom of God." 4 Nicodemus said to him, "How can a man be born when he is old? Can he enter the second time into his mother's womb and be born?" 5 Jesus answered, "Truly, truly, I say to you, unless one is born of water and the Spirit, he cannot enter the kingdom of God. 6 That which is born of the flesh is flesh, and that which is born of the Spirit is spirit. 7 Do not marvel that I said to you, 'You must be born anew.' 8 The wind blows where it wills, and you hear the sound of it, but you do not know whence it comes or whither it goes; so it is with every one who is born of the Spirit." 9 Nicodemus said to him, "How can this be?" 10 Jesus answered him, "Are you a teacher of Israel, and yet you do not understand this? 11 Truly, truly, I say to you, we speak of what we know, and bear witness to what we have seen; but you do not receive our testimony. 12 If I have told you earthly things and you do not believe, how can you believe if I tell you heavenly things? 13 No one has ascended into heaven but he who descended from heaven, the Son of man. 14 And as Moses lifted up the serpent in the wilderness, so must the Son of man be lifted up, 15 that whoever believes in him may have eternal life."

The well and the woman
of Samaria

John 4. 1 – 42 (RSV)

Now when the Lord knew that the Pharisees had heard that Jesus was making and baptising more disciples than John 2 (although Jesus himself did not baptise but only his disciples), he left Judea and departed again to Galilee. 4 He had to pass through Samaria. So he came to a city of Samaria called Sychar, near the field that Jacob gave to his son Joseph. 6 Jacob's well was there, and so Jesus, wearied as he was with his journey, sat down beside the well. It was about the sixth hour.

7 There came a woman of Samaria to draw water. Jesus said to her, "Give me a drink." 8 For his disciples had gone away into the city to buy food. 9 The Samaritan woman said to him, "How is it that you, a Jew, ask a drink of me, a woman of Samaria?" For Jews have no dealings with Samaritans. 10 Jesus answered her, "If you knew the gift of God, and who it is that is saying to you, 'Give me a drink,' you would have asked him, and he would have given you living water." 11 The woman said to him, "Sir, you have nothing to draw with, and the well is deep; where do you get that living water? Are you greater than our father Jacob who gave us the well and drank from it himself, and his sons, and

his cattle?" 13 Jesus said to her, "Every one who drinks of this water will thirst again, 14 but whoever drinks of the water that I shall give him will never thirst; the water that I shall give him will become in him a spring of water welling up to eternal life." 15 The woman said to him, "Sir, give me this water, that I may not thirst, nor come here to draw."

16 Jesus said to her, "Go, call your husband, and come here." 17 The woman answered him, "I have no husband"; Jesus said to her, "You are right in saying, 'I have no husband'; for you have had five husbands, and he whom you now have is not your husband; this you said truly." 19 The woman said to him, "Sir, I perceive that you are a prophet. 20 Our fathers worshipped on this mountain; and you say that in Jerusalem is the place where men ought to worship." 21 and Jesus said to her, "Woman, believe me, the hour is coming when neither on this mountain nor in Jerusalem will you worship the Father. 22 You worship what you do not know; we worship what we know, for salvation is from the Jews. 23 But the hour is coming, and now is, when the true worshippers will worship the Father in spirit and truth, for such the Father seeks to worship him. 24 God is spirit, and those who worship him must worship in spirit and truth." 25 The woman said to him, "I know that Messiah is coming (he who is called Christ); when he comes, he will show us all things." 26 Jesus said to her, "I who speak to you

am he."

27 Just then his disciples came. They marvelled that he was talking with a woman, but none said, "What do you wish?" or "Why are you talking with her?" 28 So the woman left her water jar, and went away into the city, and said to the people, 29 "Come, see a man who told me all that I ever did. Can this be the Christ?" 30 They went out of the city and were coming to him

31 Meanwhile the disciples besought him, saying, "Rabbi, eat." 32 But he said to them, "I have food to eat of which you do not know." 33 So the disciples said to one another, "Has any one brought him food?" 34 Jesus said to them, "My food is to do the will of him who sent me, and to accomplish his work. 35 Do you not say, 'There are yet four months, then comes the harvest'? I tell you, lift your eyes, and see how the fields are already white for harvest. 36 He who reaps receives wages, and gathers fruit for eternal life, so that sower and reaper may rejoice together. 37 For here the saying holds true, 'One sows and another reaps.' 38 I sent you to reap that for which you did not labour; others have laboured, and you have entered into their labour."

39 Many Samaritans from that city believed in him because of the woman's testimony, "He told me all that I ever did." 40 So when the Samaritans came to him, they asked him to stay with them; and he stayed there two days. 41 And many more

believed because of his word. 42 They said to the woman, "It is no longer because of your words that we believe, for we have heard for ourselves, and we know that this is indeed the Saviour of the world.

Compassion for the people. The harvest is plentiful

Matthew 9 35 – 38 (RSV)

35 and Jesus went about all the cities and villages, teaching in their synagogues and preaching the gospel of the kingdom, and healing every disease and every infirmity. 36 When he saw the crowds, he had compassion for them, because they were harassed and helpless, like sheep without a shepherd. 37 Then he said to his disciples, "The harvest is plentiful, but the labourers are few; 38 pray therefore the Lord of the harvest to send out labourers into his harvest."

Chapter VIII

Appointing the apostles

Matthew 10. 1 – 42   (RSV)

And he called to him his twelve disciples and gave them authority over unclean spirits, to cast them out, and to heal every disease and every infirmity . 2 The names of the twelve apostles are these; first, Simon, who is called Peter, and Andrew his brother; James the son of Zebedee, and John his brother; 3 Philip and Bartholomew; Thomas and Matthew the tax collector; James the son of Alphaeus, and Thaddaeus; 4   Simon the Canaanean, and Judas Iscariot, who betrayed him.

5   These twelve Jesus sent out, charging them, "Go nowhere among the Gentiles, and enter no town of the Samaritans, 6 but go rather to the lost sheep of the house of Israel. 7   And preach as you go, saying, "The kingdom of heaven is at hand." 8 Heal the sick, raise the dead, cleanse lepers, cast out demons. You received without paying, give without pay. 9 Take no gold, nor silver, nor copper in your belt, 10 no bag for your journey, nor two tunics, nor sandals, nor staff; for the labourer deserves his food. 11 And whatever town or village you enter, find out

who is worthy in it, and stay with him until you depart. 12 As you enter the house salute it. 13 And if the house is worthy, let your peace come upon it; but if it is not worthy, let your peace return to you. 14 And if anyone will not receive you or listen to your words, shake off the dust from your feet as you leave that house or town. 15 Truly I say to you, it shall be more tolerable on the day of judgement for the land of Sodom and Gomorrah than for that town.

16 "Behold, I send you out as sheep in the midst of wolves; so be wise as serpents and innocent as doves. 17 Beware of men; for they will deliver you up to councils, and flog you in their synagogues, 18 and you will be dragged before governors and kings for my sake, to bear testimony before them and the Gentiles. 19 When they deliver you up, do not be anxious how you are to speak or what you are to say; for what you are to say will be given to you in that hour; 20 for it is not you who speak but the Spirit of your Father speaking through you. 21 Brother will deliver up brother to death, and the father his child, and children will rise against parents and have them put to death; 22 and you will be hated by all for my name's sake. But he who endures to the end will be saved. 23 When they persecute you in one town, flee to the next; for truly, I say to you, you will not have gone through all the towns of Israel, before the Son of Man comes.

24 "A disciple is not above his teacher, nor a

servant above his master; 25 it is enough for the disciple to be like his teacher, and the servant like his master. If they have called the master of the house Beelzebub, how much more will they malign those of his household.

26 "So have no fear of them; for nothing is covered that will not be revealed, or hidden that will not be known. 27 What I tell you in the dark, utter in the light; and what you hear whispered, proclaim upon the housetops. 28 And do not fear those who kill the body but cannot kill the soul; rather fear him who can destroy both soul and body in hell. 29 Are not two sparrows sold for a penny? And not one of them will fall to the ground without your Father's will. 30 But even the hairs of your head are all numbered. 31 Fear not, therefore; you are of more value than many sparrows. 32 So everyone who acknowledges me before men, I also will acknowledge before my Father who is in heaven; 33 but whoever denies me before men, I also will deny before my Father who is in heaven.

34 "Do not think that I have come to bring peace on earth; I have not come to bring peace but a sword. 35 For I have come to set a man against his father, and a daughter against her mother, and a daughter-in-law against her mother-in-law; 36 and a man's foes will be those of his own household. 37 He who loves father or mother more than me is not worthy of me; and he who loves son or daughter

more than me is not worthy of me; 38 and he who does not take his cross and follow me is not worthy of me. 39 He who finds his life will lose it, and he who loses his life for my sake will find it.

40 "He who receives you receives me, and he who receives me receives him who sent me. 41 He who receives a prophet because he is a prophet shall receive a prophet's reward, and he who receives a righteous man because he is a righteous man shall receive a righteous man's reward. 42 And whoever gives to one of these little ones even a cup of cold water because he is a disciple, truly, I say to you, he shall not lose his reward."

It's an extraordinary idea, really, Christ calling together and commissioning his special disciples and then sending them off on their own to get on with his work of healing and teaching, with a daunting description of freedom from encumbrances.

The crunch moment has arrived. They must summon all the faith, all the strength they have gathered from their daily association with Jesus and, on their own, set out to put into practice the ministry they profess to believe in. No doubts or fears on their part are recorded, and, as far as we understand it, when later they come back to report, they are not without successes to recount.

A bumpy ride is portrayed, part of the uncosiness of following Christ. But in fact all we are asked to do is to be true to our truest selves in the depths of our being. The problems start in the encounter with the world around, vested interests, our own most of all, of course, powerblocs, ways of life that feel threatened by the simplicity of our true selves.

Jesus preaching. John sends his disciples

Matthew 11 1 – 30   (RSV)
And when Jesus had finished instructing his twelve disciples, he went on from there to teach and preach in their cities.

2   Now when John heard in prison about the deeds of the Christ, he sent word by his disciples 3 and said to him, "Are you he who is to come, or shall we look for another?" 4 And Jesus answered them "Go and tell John what you hear and see: 5   the blind receive their sight and the lame walk, lepers are cleansed and the deaf hear, and the dead are raised up, and the poor have good news preached to them. 6 And blessed is he who takes no offence at me."

7 As they went away, Jesus began to speak to the crowds concerning John: "What did you go out into the wilderness to behold? A reed shaken by the wind? 8 Why then did you go out? To see a man

clothed in soft raiment? Behold, those who wear soft raiment are in kings' houses. 9 Why then did you go out? To see a prophet? Yes I tell you and more than a prophet. 10 This is he of whom it is written

'Behold, I send my messenger before thy face
who shall prepare thy way before thee'

11 Truly, I say to you, among those born of women there has risen no one greater than John the Baptist: yet he who is least in the kingdom of heaven is greater than he. 12 From the days of John the Baptist until now the kingdom of heaven has suffered violence, and men of violence take it by force. 13 For all the prophets and the law prophesied until John; 14 and if you are willing to accept it he is Elijah who is to come. 15 He who has ears to hear, let him hear. 16 "But to what shall I compare this generation? It is like children sitting in the marketplaces and calling to their playmates,

17 'We piped to you, and you did not dance;

we wailed to you and you did not mourn.'

18 For John came neither eating nor drinking, and they say, 'He has a demon'; 19 The Son of Man came eating and drinking, and they say, 'Behold a glutton and a drunkard, a friend of tax collectors and sinners!' Yet wisdom is justified by her deeds"

20 Then he began to upbraid the cities where most of his mighty works had been done, because they did not repent. 21 "Woe to you, Chorazin! Woe

to you, Bethsaida! For if the mighty works done in you had been done in Tyre & Sidon they would have repented long ago in sackcloth and ashes. 22 But I tell you, it shall be more tolerable on the day of judgement for Tyre and Sidon than for you. 23 And you Capernaum, will you be exalted to heaven? You shall be brought down to Hades. For if the mighty works done in you had been done in Sodom, it would have remained until this day. 24 But I tell you that it shall be more tolerable on the day of judgement for the land of Sodom than for you."

25 At that time Jesus declared, "I thank thee, Father, Lord of heaven and earth, that thou hast hid these things from the wise and understanding and revealed them to babes; 26 yea Father for such was thy gracious will. 27 All things have been delivered to me by my Father; and no one knows the Son except the Father, and no one knows the Father except the Son and any one to whom the Son chooses to reveal him. 28 Come to me, all who labour and are heavy laden, and I will give you rest. 29 Take my yoke upon you and learn from me; for I am gentle and lowly in heart, and you will find rest for your souls. 30 For my yoke is easy, and my burden is light."

Disciples eating grain from cornfields

Mark 2 23 – 28   (RSV)

23   One sabbath he was going through the grain fields; and as they made their way his disciples began to pluck heads of grain.   24   And the Pharisees said to him, "Look, why are they doing what is not lawful on the sabbath?" 25 And he said to them, "Have you never read what David did, when he was in need and was hungry, he and those who were with him; 26 how he entered the house of God when Abiathar was high priest and ate the bread of the Presence, which is not lawful for any but the priests to eat, and also gave it to those who were with him?" 27 And he said to them, "The sabbath was made for man not man for the sabbath; 28 so the Son of man is Lord even of the sabbath."

Man with withered hand

Matthew 12 9 – 14   (RSV)

9   And he went on from there, and entered their synagogue. 10 And behold, there was a man with a withered hand. And they asked him, "Is it lawful to heal on the sabbath?" so that they might accuse him.

11 He said to them, "What man of you, if he has one sheep and it falls into a pit on the sabbath, will not lay hold of it and lift it out? 12 Of how much more value is a man than a sheep! So it is lawful to do good on the sabbath." 13 Then he said to the man, "Stretch out your hand." And the man stretched it out, and it was restored, whole like the other. 14 But the Pharisees went out and took counsel against him, how to destroy him.

In his own country

Mark 6 1 – 13 (RSV)

He went away from there and came to his own country; and his disciples followed him. 2 And on the sabbath he began to teach in the synagogue; and many who heard him were astonished, saying, "Where did this man get all this? What is the wisdom given to him? What mighty works are wrought by his hands! 3 Is not this the carpenter, the son of Mary and brother of James and Joses and Judas and Simon, and are not his sisters here with us?" And they took offence at him. 4 And Jesus said to them, "A prophet is not without honour, except in his own country, and among his own kin, and in his own house." 5 And he could do no mighty works, except that he laid his hands upon a few sick people and healed them. 6 And he marvelled because of their unbelief.

And he went about among the villages teaching.

Pool at Bethzatha

John 5. 1 – 18 (RSV)
After this there was a feast of the Jews, and Jesus went up to Jerusalem.

2 Now there is in Jerusalem by the Sheep Gate a pool, in Hebrew called Bethzatha, which has five porticoes. 3 In these lay a multitude of invalids, blind, lame, paralysed. 5 One man was there, who had been ill for thirty-eight years. 6 When Jesus saw him and knew that he had been lying there a long time, he said to him, "Do you want to be healed?" 7 The sick man answered him, "Sir I have no man to put me into the pool when the water is troubled, and while I am going another steps down before me." 8 Jesus said to him, "Rise take up your pallet, and walk." 9 And at once the man was healed, and he took up his pallet and walked.

Now that day was the sabbath. 10 So the Jews said to the man who was cured "It is the sabbath, it is not lawful for you to carry your pallet." 11 But he answered them, "The man who healed me said to me, 'Take up your pallet, and walk'" 12 They asked him, "Who is the man who said to you, 'Take up your pallet, and walk ?'" 13 Now the man who had been healed did not know who it was, for Jesus had withdrawn, as there was a crowd in the place. 14 Afterward, Jesus found him in the temple, and said to him, "See you are well! Sin no more, that nothing worse befall you." 15 The man went away and told the Jews that it was Jesus who had healed him. 16 And this was why the Jews persecuted Jesus, because he did this on the sabbath. 17 But Jesus answered them, "My Father is working still, and I am working." 18 This was why the Jews sought all the more to kill him, because he not only broke the sabbath but also called God his own Father, making himself equal with God.

Herod, Salome, killing of John

Mark 6 14 – 29   (RSV)

14   King Herod heard of it: for Jesus name had become known. Some said, "John the baptiser has been raised from the dead; that is why these powers are working in him". 15 But others said "It is Elijah" And others said, "It is a prophet, like one of the prophets of old." 16 But when Herod heard of it he said, "John whom I beheaded has been raised." For Herod had sent and seized John, and bound him in

108

prison for the sake of Herodias his brother Phillip's wife; because he had married her. 18 For John said to Herod, "It is not lawful for you to have your brother's wife." 19 And Herodias had a grudge against him and wanted to kill him. But she could not 20 for Herod feared John, knowing that he was a righteous holy man, and kept him safe. When he heard him he was much perplexed; and yet he heard him gladly, 21 But an opportunity came when Herod on his birthday gave a banquet for his courtiers and officers and the leading men of Galilee. 22 For when Herodias' daughter came in and danced, she pleased Herod and his guests; and the king said to the girl, "Ask me for whatever you wish and I will grant it." 23 And he vowed to her, "Whatever you ask me, I will give you, even half of my kingdom." 24 And she went out, and said to her mother, "What shall I ask?" And she said,"The head of John the baptiser. " 25 And she came in immediately with haste to the King and asked saying, "I want you to give me at once the head of John the Baptist on a platter." 26 And the king was exceedingly sorry; but because of his oaths and his guests he did not want to break his word to her. 27 And immediately the king sent a soldier of the guard and gave orders to bring his head. He went and beheaded him in the prison, 28 and brought his head on a platter, and gave it to the girl; and the girl gave it to her mother. 29 When his disciples heard of it, they came and took his body, and laid it in a tomb.

Chapter IX
Disciples coming back to report. Feeding of the 5,000

Mark 6 30 – 44   (RSV)

30 The Apostles returned to Jesus, and told him all that they had done and taught. 31 And he said to them, "Come away by yourselves to a lonely place, and rest awhile." For many were coming and going, and they had no leisure even to eat. 32 And they went away in the boat to a lonely place by themselves. 33 Now many saw them going, and knew them, and they ran there on foot from all the towns, and got there ahead of them. 34 As he went ashore he saw a great throng, and he had compassion on them, because they were like sheep without a shepherd; and he began to teach them many things. 35 And when it grew late, his disciples came to him and said, "This is a lonely place, and the hour is now late; 36 Send them away to go into the country and villages roundabout and buy themselves something to eat." 37 But he answered them, "You give them something to eat." And they

said to him, "Shall we go and buy two hundred denarii worth of bread, and give it them to eat?" 38 And he said to them, "How many loaves have you? Go and see." And when they had found out, they said, "Five, and two fish." 39 Then he commanded them all to sit down by companies upon the green grass. 40 So they sat down in groups, by hundreds and by fifties. 41 And taking the five loaves and the two fish he looked up to heaven, and blessed, and broke the loaves, and gave them to the disciples to set before the people; and he divided the two fish among them all. 42 And they all ate and were satisfied. 43 And they took up twelve baskets full of broken pieces and of the fish. 44 And those who ate the loaves were five thousand men.

The disciples come back to report on the results of their amazing challenge of, on their own, attempting to deliver Christ's ministry of healing and teaching.

From the absence of any recorded criticism from Jesus for failure of faith or nerve, we must assume they came back not unattended with success. Indeed in Luke Chapter 10 Verse 17 the "seventy" Luke refers to as having been sent out he reports returning 'with joy, saying: "Lord, even the demons are subject to us in your name!"'

Amazing indeed. Christ, indeed, is compassionate to them, proposing they should get away together to rest. Some clergy like to present the feeding of the

5,000 as the miracle of sharing. 5,000 people have come together in an impromptu gathering on a remote hillside.

The disciples point out to Jesus that they will need to eat and suggest he send them off to get food for themselves. Jesus responds by simply telling his disciples that they should feed them instead. In response to their reasonable query as to how they are expected to do that he calls for what supplies they have – five loaves and two small fishes that a local boy is enterprisingly offering for sale.

Blessing and breaking these provisions in front of the 5000 he publicly gives to them all he has, shaming them to reach inside their shirts and pull out the hasty provisions they had grabbed before running from home and stuffed out of sight for their personal use later. All are filled and more than filled.

It is an attractive idea; an allegory for our world and its problems; how they could fundamentally all be addressed if we were simply ready to put our hand inside our shirt and genuinely share our resources.

Jesus could not have known whether or not the solution to the problem lay indeed under the shirts of the people before him. He simply takes what he has and puts it into the hands of God.

Sending disciples away in boat.

Going up mountain to pray.
Rejoining disciples.
Walking on water

Matthew 14. 22 – 33   (RSV)

22 Then he made the disciples get into the boat and go before him to the other side, while he dismissed the crowds. 23   And after he had dismissed the crowds, he went up on the mountain by himself to pray. When evening came, he was there alone, 24 but the boat by this time was many furlongs distant from the land, beaten by the waves; for the wind was against them. 25   And in the fourth watch of the night, he came to them, walking on the sea. 26 But when the disciples saw him walking on the sea, they were terrified, saying, "It is a ghost!" And they cried out for fear. 27 But immediately he spoke to them, saying, "Take heart, it is I; have no fear." 28 And Peter answered him, "Lord if it is you, bid me come to you on the water." 29 He said, "Come." So Peter got out of the boat and walked on the water and came to Jesus; 30 but when he saw the wind, he was afraid, and beginning to sink he cried out, "Lord, save me." 31   Jesus immediately reached out his hand and caught him saying to him ,"O man of little faith, why did you doubt?" 32 And when they got into the boat, the wind ceased. 33 And those in the

boat worshipped him saying, "Truly you are the Son
of God."

The miracle recorded here is, I think, unique in that
it is not related to any act of healing or caring, but
simply to the transcendence in everything of God.
Jesus, rejoining his disciples, is not to be interrupted
by the laws of nature.

One feels such sympathy with Peter. The leap of
faith followed, at just the wrong moment, by its
panicked loss. Jesus' strong hand is needed to pull
him back.

Gennesaret. Sick brought

Mark 6. 53 – 55 (RSV)

53 And when they had crossed over, they came to
land at Gennesaret, and moored to the shore. 54
And when they got out of the boat, immediately the
people recognised him, 55 and ran about the whole
neighbourhood, and began to bring sick people on
their pallets to any place where they heard he was.

They are so affecting, the accounts of people in their
desperation to get near Jesus, and how that affects
him. In the feeding of the 5,000 – 'And they went
away in a boat to a lonely place by themselves. Now

many saw them going and knew them, and they ran there on foot from all the towns, and got there ahead of them. As he went ashore he saw a great throng, and he had compassion on them, because they were like sheep without a shepherd.'

And here – 'Immediately the people recognised him and ran about the whole neighbourhood and began to bring sick people on their pallets to any place where they heard he was.'

Pharisees – why do your disciples not observe tradition?

Mark 7. 1 – 23 (RSV)

Now when the Pharisees gathered together to him, with some of the scribes, who had come from Jerusalem, 2 they saw that some of his disciples ate with hands defiled, that is unwashed. 3 (For the Pharisees, and all the Jews, do not eat unless they wash their hands, observing the tradition of the elders; 4 and when they come from the marketplace, they do not eat unless they purify themselves; and there are many other traditions which they observe, the washing of cups and pots and vessels of bronze). 5 And the Pharisees and the scribes asked him, "Why do your disciples not live according to the tradition of the elders, but eat with hands defiled?" 6 And he said to them, "Well did Isaiah prophesy of you hypocrites as it is written

'This people honours me with their lips,

But their heart is far from me;

7 in vain do they worship me,

teaching as doctrines the precepts of men.'

8 You leave the commandment of God, and hold fast the tradition of men"

9 And he said to them, "You have a fine way of rejecting the commandment of God, in order to keep your tradition! 10 For Moses said, 'Honour your father and your mother; and, 'He who speaks evil of father or mother, let him surely die'; 11 but you say, 'If a man tells his father or his mother, What you would have gained from me is Corban (that is, given to God) - 12 then you no longer permit him to do anything for his father or mother, 13 thus making void the word of God through your tradition which you hand on. And many such things you do."

14 And he called the people to him again, and said to them,"Hear me, all of you, and understand: 15 there is nothing outside a man which by going into him can defile him; but the things which come out of the man are what defile him." 16 If any man has ears to hear let him hear." 17 And when he had entered the house, and left the people, his disciples asked him about the parable. 18 And he said to them, "Then are you also without understanding? Do you not see that whatever goes into a man from

outside cannot defile him, 19 since it enters not his heart but his stomach, and so passes on?" (Thus he declared all foods clean.) 20 And he said, "What comes out of a man is what defiles a man. 21 For from within, out of the heart of man, come evil thoughts, fornication, theft, murder, adultery, 22 coveting, wickedness, deceit, licentiousness, envy, slander, pride, foolishness. 23 All these evil things come from within and they defile a man."

The Canaanite woman

Matthew 15 21 – 28   (RSV)

21 And Jesus went away from there and withdrew to the district of Tyre and Sidon. 22 And behold, a Canaanite woman from that region came out and cried, "Have mercy on me Lord, Son of David; my daughter is severely possessed by a demon." 23 But he did not answer her a word. And his disciples came and begged him saying, "Send her away, for she is crying after us." 24 He answered, "I was sent only to the lost sheep of the house of Israel." 25 But she came and knelt before him saying, "Lord help me." 26 And he answered, "It is not fair to take the children's bread and throw it to the dogs." 27 She said, "Yes, Lord, yet even the dogs eat the crumbs that fall from their masters' table." 28 Jesus

answered her, "O woman, great is your faith! Be it done for you as you desire." And her daughter was healed instantly.

We are so used to Christ's message and his sacrifice being for *us*, it comes as a bit of a shock to think that we might not have been included in his original plans for his ministry. But if the message Christ felt himself entrusted to deliver was to be delivered to the world it had to be delivered through a suitable medium; a medium that already had the language and the capacity to accommodate and engage with the ideas put forward by him.

Arguably Judaism was the only possible starting point from which Christ's call for total personal relationship with God could be developed. Buddhism, which overlaid so much of the central Christian vision, did not admit of the concept of God. Hinduism – a complex multiplicity of deities. Islam was not yet born. Where to start with paganism? Judaism began already with an advanced concept of a personal relationship between God and man, although perhaps more focussed, apart from a few chosen servants, on God's people as a whole rather than on individuals.

The ten Commandments provided both a profound guide for an individual's moral and spiritual growth and well-being, and rules to make it possible for humanity to live together in respect for each other; the first few focussing on the spiritual, the place that God should have in every person's life, with the ultimately civilised recognition that for mental, spiritual, and physical health and well-being time had to be set aside for the inner person and all that contained, ring-fenced against all normal preoccupations and activities (the sabbath); then the call to view one's neighbour not just with respect but with the same love borne for yourself; respect for the family; some absolutely basic rules for living together – you shall not kill, you shall not commit adultery, you shall not steal, you shall not bear false witness; and ending with a reversion to a moral and spiritual code for every individual. You shall not only not take your neighbour's wife or any of his possessions, you must not allow yourself to even want to take them; all of which reflected a treasure of gathered wisdom and understanding of human nature.

The Old Testament God of these laws for living, however fair he may have been, did display a number of rather human characteristics e.g. a tendency to get (no doubt entirely reasonably) very angry when let down or thwarted by his chosen people, with punishment and revenge, in the form of the misfortunes experienced by the Jewish people, often unleashed in consequence.

By Jesus' time the treasure of rabbinical study and thought would certainly have moved the view of that God to one where he would be recognised as caring for his chosen people even when they let him down, but the God Jesus announced was a God of absolute, infinite, and all-encompassing love, longing for union with his children, with no sin so great, or moment so late that true repentance would not bring immediate remission and a place at God's side.

This message was welcomed by many devout followers of Judaism. For many engaged in its administration, however, among the Chief Priests, scribes, Pharisees, the message was viewed rather differently. The only control relevant now for followers was God's will. The only function now for the temple hierarchy was the setting of example in their lives.

The greatest could only manifest themselves by the humblest service of others. Power, privilege, wealth were swept away at a breath. The Temple authorities had a very clear choice to make; hand over control and participate in what could be the ultimate fulfilment of the law and the prophets; or resist the message to the end.

Jesus' understanding of his mission, therefore, was to introduce those missing elements to Judaism, purge it of the abuses and hypocrisies that had inevitably accumulated in a bureaucratic administration, which, then, as a sanctified and fully developed instrument could now be used to deliver the message to the world as a whole; but first the message was to Judaism and the Jews. At the end, though, Jesus could never say no to a sincere appeal for his help. And so the Canaanite woman came to be included in his ministry, and, by extension, all of us. No one was ever more than one call away from him.

Chapter X
Parable of the lost sheep

Luke 15 1 – 10 (RSV)

Now the tax collectors and sinners were all drawing near to hear him. 2 And the Pharisees and the scribes murmured, saying, "This man receives sinners and eats with them."

3 So he told them this parable: 4 "What man of you, having a hundred sheep, if he has lost one of them, does not leave the ninety nine in the wilderness, and go after the one which is lost, until he finds it? 5 And when he has found it, he lays it on his shoulders, rejoicing. 6 And when he comes home, he calls together his friends and his neighbours, saying to them, 'Rejoice with me, for I have found my sheep which was lost.' Just so, I tell you, there will be more joy in heaven over one sinner who repents than over ninety nine righteous persons who need no repentance.

8 "Or what woman, having ten silver coins, if she loses one coin, does not light a lamp and sweep the house and seek diligently until she finds it? 9 And when she has found it, she calls together her friends and neighbours saying, 'Rejoice with me, for I have

found the coin which I had lost.' 10 Just so, I tell you, there is joy before the Angels of God over one sinner who repents.

Parable of the prodigal son

Luke 15. 11 – 32 (RSV)

11 And he said, "There was a man who had two sons; 12 and the younger of them said to his father, 'Father, give me the share of property that falls to me.' And he divided his living between them. 13 Not many days later, the younger son gathered all he had and took his journey into a far country, and there he squandered his property in loose living. 14 And when he had spent everything, a great famine arose in that country, and he began to be in want. 15 So he went and joined himself to one of the citizens of that country, who sent him into his fields to feed swine. 16 And he would gladly have fed on the pods that the swine ate; and no one gave him anything. 17 But when he came to himself he said, "How many of my father's hired servants have bread enough and to spare, but I perish here with hunger! 18 I will arise and go to my father, and I will say to him, "Father I have sinned against heaven and before you; 19 I am no longer worthy to be called your son; treat me as one of your hired servants."

20 And he arose and came to his father. But while he was yet at a distance, his father saw him and had compassion, and ran and embraced him and kissed him. 21 And the son said to him, 'Father, I have sinned against heaven and before you; I am no longer worthy to be called your son.' 22 But the father said to his servants, 'Bring quickly the best robe, and put it on him; and put a ring on his hand, and shoes on his feet; 23 and bring the fatted calf and kill it and let us eat and make merry; 24 for this my son was dead, and is alive again; he was lost, and is found'. And they began to make merry.

25 "Now his elder son was in the field; and as he came and drew near to the house, he heard music and dancing. 26 And he called one of the servants and asked what this meant. 27 And he said to him, 'Your brother has come, and your Father has killed the fatted calf, because he has received him safe and sound.' 28 But he was angry and refused to go in. His father came out and entreated him, 29 but he answered his father, 'Lo these many years I have served you, and I never disobeyed your command; yet you never gave me a kid, that I might make merry with my friends. 30 But when this son of yours came, who has devoured your living with harlots, you killed for him the fatted calf! 31 And he said to him, "Son, you are always with me, and all that is mine is yours. 32 It was fitting to make merry and be glad, for this your brother was dead, and is

alive; he was lost, and is found.'"

One does sympathise a bit with the elder son when he says "Lo these many years I have served you, and I never disobeyed your command; yet you never gave me a kid, that I might make merry with my friends."

Yet he already has been living in the company of God, with all the joy, freedom, and fulfilment that make that up, and with the prospect of full inheritance of the kingdom. What of worth can be added to that? The celebrations are for someone who has so far denied himself these things, and can now start to taste them.

The rich man and Lazarus, the poor man

Luke 16 19 – 31   (RSV)

19   "There was a rich man, who was clothed in purple and fine linen and who feasted sumptuously every day. 20 and at his gate lay a poor man named Lazarus, full of sores, 21 who desired to be fed with what fell from the rich man's table; moreover the dogs came and licked his sores. 22 The poor man died and was carried by the angels to Abraham's bosom. The rich man also died and was buried; and in Hades, being in torment, he lifted up

his eyes, and saw Abraham far off and Lazarus in his bosom. 24 And he called out, 'Father Abraham, have mercy upon me, and send Lazarus to dip the end of his finger in water and cool my tongue; for I am in anguish in this flame.' 25 But Abraham said, 'Son, remember that you in your lifetime received your good things, and Lazarus in like manner evil things; but now he is comforted here and you are in anguish. 26 And besides all this, between us and you a great chasm has been fixed, in order that those who would pass from here to you may not be able, and none may cross from there to us.' 27 And he said, 'Then I beg you, father, to send him to my father's house, 28 for I have five brothers, so that he may warn them, lest they also come into this place of torment.' 29 But Abraham said, 'They have Moses and the prophets; let them hear them.' 30 And he said, 'No, father Abraham; but if some one goes to them from the dead, they will repent.' 31 He said to him, 'If they do not hear Moses and the prophets, neither will they be convinced if some one should rise from the dead.'"

Jesus' reference in his parables to hell have long since made no sense to me. One scintilla of the love to be found at the bottom of your heart raises impossible incompatibilities for revenge and torment.

For Jesus and his disciples, this would have been

the language of their religion. Also, Jesus' call to make spiritual rather than material the main focus of your life was, in an age of a daily tooth and nail, every man for himself struggle for survival, potentially a call to put that survival on the line.

The rewards for making that choice had not only to be compellingly stated, but fairly graphic descriptions also given of the results of not making it. Jesus' terrifying descriptions of hell and damnation are of course balanced throughout his teaching by the constant reference to God's overwhelming love for and longing for communion with *all* his creation, saints and sinners, and his instant and all-embracing forgiveness for anyone who genuinely turns to him, no matter how late – the Prodigal Son, The Labourers hired at the eleventh hour, the Shepherd leaving his 99 sheep to find and return rejoicing with, on his shoulders, the missing one.

Perhaps the omission of reference to the threat of a tortured hell would have been one step too far, too soon to be assimilated in addition to everything else, weakening rather than strengthening the concept of the all-loving, all forgiving God, giving the misleading impression of a shapeless 'Anything goes' situation. No need to worry about what sort of life you led as long as your repentance was in at the end in time.

In fact, true repentance involves a profound

emotional and mental acknowledgement, change, and commitment, not open for triggering by a quick tactical 'Sorry'. That repentance is not required for God's forgiveness. We have that already. It is needed for ourselves, to free us for union with him. The incredibly powerful stories of forgiveness in the *Forgiveness Project's 'f' word exhibition* includes one from a chronically injured victim of a hit and run incident who found it in himself to forgive the driver who has never been traced.

"Some people," he says, "in the church believe you can't forgive unless the other person repents, but to me repentance is'nt a condition of forgiveness because ultimately forgiveness comes from within." A human is capable of such unconditional forgiveness and not God?

It perhaps needed a bit of time and experience to recognise the hell of emptiness of absence and separation from the God Jesus had brought forward.

Abraham's apparently pitiless rejection of the rich man's plea, first to send Lazarus to him to relieve him in his suffering, and then to warn his brothers and family – "There is a great chasm between us; - and – "If they do not hear Moses and the prophets..." – is only a simple reflection of the facts.

There is indeed a chasm between someone who has focused throughout their life on the development of their spirit and someone who has not, bridgeable only by the person who has not, and as regards warning his family – "If some one goes to them from the dead they will repent" – all the evidence points conclusively to the contrary – 'For even his brothers did not believe in him' (John 7 1-5), and 'Woe to you, Chorasin! Woe to you Bethsaida!' (Matthew 11. 20 – 24).

My angle on the difference between someone who has tried to develop their spiritual life and someone who has not is fundamentally one of missed opportunity; the opportunity to embark on the greatest adventure possible, finding and attempting to become your true full self, with all the glory of richness that involves. What could compare with that?

For all my feeble efforts in that direction so far, I thank God in his mercy that he didn't have me born with villas and yachts. I am very dubious that I would ever have been strong enough to stop their being the main focus of my life.

Many years ago I saw a picture I have never forgotten. It was in some book of famous photographs. It was of a boy in rags, dancing, in Naples I think, some time after the Second World War. Of possessions he obviously had none, but the radiant happiness that streamed from every part of him literally stopped your breath. If ever there was a photograph of the Kingdom of Heaven on earth, that was it.

I wish I knew where to find it now.

Chapter XI
We only do

Luke 17 1 – 10 (RSV)

And he said to his disciples,"Temptations to sin are sure to come; but woe to him by whom they come! 2 It would be better for him if a millstone were hung round his neck and he were cast into the sea, than that he should cause one of these little ones to sin. 3   Take heed to yourselves; if your brother sins rebuke him and if he repents, forgive him; 4 and if he sins against you seven times in the day, and turns to you seven times, and says, 'I repent' you must forgive him."

5   The apostles said to the Lord, "Increase our faith!" 6   And the Lord said, "If you had faith as a grain of mustard seed, you could say to this sycamine tree, 'Be rooted up, and be planted in the sea,' and it would obey you.

7   "Will any one of you, who has a servant ploughing or keeping sheep, say to him when he has come in from the field, 'Come at once and sit down at table'? 8 Will he not rather say to him, 'Prepare supper for me, and gird yourself and serve me, till I eat and drink; and afterward you shall eat and drink'? 9 Does he thank the servant because he did

what was commanded? 10 So you also, when you have done all that is commanded you, say, 'We are unworthy servants; we have only done what was our duty.'"

We are reminded, in Jesus' reference to a servant, not to confuse any overcoming of our difficulties in responding to God's call with our having made some righteous sacrifice.

Surrounded as we are in God's limitless and unearned love, any response we give to that love is simply the bare minimum the situation cries out for.

Kingdom of God

Luke 17 20 – 21   (RSV)
20 Being asked by the Pharisees when the kingdom of God was coming, he answered them, "The kingdom of God is not coming with signs to be observed; 21 Nor will they say, 'Lo, here it is!' or 'There!' for behold, the kingdom of God is in the midst of you.

This seems to me to apply to all references to the Kingdom of God. It is there to be individually experienced by all of us. The end of the world is encountered by each of us when we die, with Christ's coming again and our union with God. We each of us already have our own individual apocalypse.

I am the bread of life

John 6 28 – 71(RSV)

28 Then they said to him, "What must we do, to be doing the works of God?" 29 Jesus answered them, "This is the work of God, that you believe in him whom he has sent." 30 So they said to him, "Then what sign do you do, that we may see, and believe you? What work do you perform? 31 Our fathers ate the manna in the wilderness; as it is written, 'He gave them bread from heaven to eat.'" 32 Jesus then said to them, "Truly, truly, I say to you, it was not Moses who gave you the bread from heaven; my Father gives you the true bread from heaven. 33 For the bread of God is that which comes down from heaven, and gives life to the world." 34 They said to him, "Lord, give us this bread always."

35 Jesus said to them, "I am the bread of life; he who comes to me shall not hunger, and he who believes in me shall never thirst. 36 But I said to you that you have seen me and yet do not believe. 37 All that the father gives me will come to me; and him who comes to me I will not cast out. 38 For I have come down from heaven, not to do my own will, but the will of him who sent me; 39 and this is the will of him who sent me, that I should lose

nothing of all that he has given me, but raise it up at the last day. 40 For this is the will of my Father, that every one who sees the Son and believes in him should have eternal life: and I will raise him up at the last day."

41 The Jews then murmured at him, because he said, "I am the bread which came down from heaven." 42 They said, "Is not this Jesus, the son of Joseph, whose father and mother we know? How does he now say, 'I have come down from heaven'?" 43 Jesus answered them, "Do not murmur among yourselves. 44 No one can come to me unless the Father who sent me draws him; and I will raise him up at the last day. 45 It is written in the prophets, 'And they shall all be taught by God.' Every one who has heard and learned from the Father comes to me. 46 Not that any one has seen the Father except him who is from God; he has seen the Father. 47 Truly, truly, I say to you, he who believes has eternal life. 48 I am the bread of life. 49 Your fathers ate the manna in the wilderness, and they died. 50 This is the bread which comes down from heaven, that a man may eat of it and not die. 51 I am the living bread which came down from heaven; if anyone eats of this bread, he will live for ever; and the bread which I shall give for the life of the world is my flesh."

52 The Jews then disputed among themselves, saying, "How can this man give us his flesh to eat?" 53 So Jesus said to them, "Truly, truly, I say to you,

unless you eat the flesh of the Son of man and drink his blood, you have no life in you; 54 he who eats my flesh and drinks my blood has eternal life, and I will raise him up at the last day. 55 For my flesh is food indeed, and my blood is drink indeed. 56 He who eats my flesh and drinks my blood abides in me, and I in him. 57 As the living Father sent me, and I live because of the Father, so he who eats me will live because of me. 58 This is the bread which came down from heaven, not such as the fathers ate and died; he who eats this bread will live for ever." 59 This he said in the synagogue, as he taught at Capernaum.

60 Many of his disciples, when they heard it, said, "This is a hard saying; who can listen to it?" 61 But Jesus, knowing in himself that his disciples murmured at it, said to them, "Do you take offence at this? 62 Then what if you were to see the Son of man ascending where he was before? 63 It is the spirit that gives life, the flesh is of no avail; the words that I have spoken to you are spirit and life. 64 But there are some of you that do not believe."" For Jesus knew from the first who those were that did not believe, and who it was that would betray him. 65 And he said, "This is why I told you that no one can come to me unless it is granted him by the Father."

66 After this many of his disciples drew back and no longer went about with him. 67 Jesus said to the

twelve, "Do you also wish to go away?" 68 Simon Peter answered him, "Lord, to whom shall we go? You have the words of eternal life; 69 and we have believed, and have come to know, that you are the Holy One of God." 70 Jesus answered them, "Did I not choose you, the twelve, and one of you is a devil? 71 He spoke of Judas the son of Simon Iscariot, for he, one of the twelve, was to betray him.

For Christians, the bread and wine of the communion service representing the body and blood of Christ are the ultimate sacraments of love expressed and given for us. Participation in taking them is, for most people, the moment of greatest sanctity they experience in church, prized and loved above all others.

But Jesus' original proposition of this must have been absolutely explosive to the Jews whom he addressed, and deliberately intended to be so.

For the Jews, blood was sacred, the life force given by God, and, as such, must be treated with the utmost reverence, carefully removed from anything that was to be eaten, and returned to God's creation, the earth. Only when this was done would any blood bearing food be Kosher to eat. Jesus' proposal, therefore, was doubly offensive because not only did he put forward, as a cardinal element of his message, that, whether symbolically or not, blood should be consumed, but that it should be, in his person as Son of God, the blood of God.

It is not enough, Jesus says, with rituals such as the removal of blood, to hold God in awe, at a safe distance. Union with Him is what is required, with the full sharing of his blood. It is not only an invitation. It is a challenge. As Jesus will have foreseen, it is too much for many of them, and they walk away. Are we all so open minded?

The deaf man

Mark 7. 31 – 37   (RSV)

31   Then he returned from the region of Tyre, and went through Sidon to the Sea of Galilee, through the region of the Decapolis. 32 And they brought to him a man who was deaf and had an impediment in his speech; and they besought him to lay his hand upon him.   33   And taking him aside from the multitude privately, he put his fingers into his ears, and he spat and touched his tongue;   34   and looking up to heaven, he sighed, and said to him "Ephphatha," that is, "Be opened."   35   And his ears were opened, his tongue was released, and he spoke plainly.   36   And he charged them to tell no one; but the more he charged them, the more zealously they proclaimed it.   37   And they were astonished beyond measure, saying, "He has done all things well; he even makes the deaf to hear and the dumb speak."

Blind man. What do you see?

Mark 8. 22 – 26 (RSV)

22 And they came to Bethsaida. And some people brought to him a blind man, and begged him to touch him. 23 And he took the blind man by the hand, and led him out of the village; and when he had spit on his eyes and laid his hands upon him, he asked him, "Do you see anything?" 24 And he looked up and said, "I see men; but they look like trees, walking." 25 Then again he laid his hands upon his eyes; and he looked intently and was restored, and saw everything clearly. 26 And he sent him away to his home, saying, "Do not even enter the village."

Is this a rare occasion when Jesus' own faith or focus faltered for a moment and he was not sure of the healing that had taken place? It would explain his asking the blind man "Do you see anything?" and to the blind man's reporting that he was seeing something, but imperfectly.

'Then again he laid his hands upon his eyes; and he looked intently and was restored, and saw everything clearly.'

Who do men say that I am?

Matthew 16. 13 – 20   (RSV)

13 Now when Jesus came into the district of Caesarea Philippi, he asked his disciples, "Who do men say that the Son of man is?" And they said, "Some say John the Baptist, others say Elijah, and others Jeremiah or one of the prophets." 15 He said to them, "But who do you say that I am?" Simon Peter replied, "You are the Christ, the Son of the living God." 17 And Jesus answered him, "Blessed are you, Simon Bar-Jona! For flesh and blood has not revealed this to you, but my Father who is in heaven. 18 And I tell you, you are Peter, and on this rock I will build my church and the powers of death shall not prevail against it. 19 I will give you the keys of the kingdom of heaven and whatever you bind on earth shall be bound in heaven, and whatever you loose on earth shall be loosed in heaven." 20 Then he strictly charged the disciples to tell no one that he was the Christ.

For the fulfilment of his mission, it was obviously vital that Jesus' disciples fully understood the true nature of his identity; an identity which, in due course would also be uncompromisingly laid before the rulers of the temple.

The timing of this, though, was critical. Once the scribes and Pharisees had been confronted with this declaration, Jesus' remaining lifespan was likely to be very short. By his own mouth he would have provided the evidence the authorities needed to find him guilty of blasphemy, for which the punishment was death. In addition, the whole of the time remaining to him would have been dominated by this one issue 'Divine or Not?' eclipsing all possibility of completing his ministry.

Until, therefore, he had completed his mission and delivered his message, it was essential that no hint of this declaration came into the hands of the scribes and Pharisees.

Get behind me, Satan!

Matthew 16. 21 – 28   (RSV)

21 from that time Jesus began to show his disciples that he must go to Jerusalem and suffer many things from the elders and chief priests and scribes, and be killed, and on the third day be raised. 22 And Peter took him and began to rebuke him, saying, "God forbid, Lord! This shall never happen to you." But he turned, and said to Peter, "Get behind me, Satan! You are a hindrance to me; for you are not on the side of God, but of men."

24   Then Jesus told his disciples, "If any man would come after me, let him deny himself and take up his cross and follow me. 25 For whoever would save his life will lose it, and whoever loses his life for my sake will find it. 26 For what will it profit a man,

if he gains the whole world and forfeits his life!? Or what shall a man give in return for his life? 27 For the Son of Man is to come with his angels in the glory of his Father, and then he will repay every man for what he has done. 28 Truly I say to you, there are some standing here who will not face death before they see the Son of man coming in his kingdom."

Poor Peter. Just after being told that he is the rock on which the faith Jesus is proclaiming will find its base, he is accused of doing the work of the devil; but if you have just screwed up your courage for the frightful ordeal that awaits you if you continue without compromise to pursue your mission, the last thing you want is someone you love trying to convince you that none of that is necessary.

Chapter XII
Transfiguration

Matthew 17. 1 – 8 (RSV)

And after six days Jesus took with him Peter and James and John his brother, and led them up a high mountain apart. 2 And he was transfigured before them, and his face shone like the sun and his garments became white as light. 3 And behold, there appeared to them Moses and Elijah, talking with him. 4 And Peter said to Jesus, "Lord, it is well that we are here; if you wish, I will make three booths here, one for you and one for Moses and one for Elijah." 5 He was still speaking, when lo, a bright cloud overshadowed them, and a voice from the cloud said, "This is my beloved son, with whom I am well pleased; listen to him." 6 When the disciples heard this, they fell on their faces, and were filled with awe. 7 But Jesus came and touched them saying, "Rise, and have no fear." 8 And when they lifted up their eyes, they saw no one but Jesus only.

Peter's words have the authentic ring of the dream-like nonsense that would be likely to come out of your mouth if you found yourself suddenly exalted into an overwhelming inspirational experience.

Disciples failing with boy with epilepsy

Matthew 17. 14 – 23   (RSV)

14 And when they came to the crowd, a man came up to him and kneeling before him said, 15 "Lord, have mercy on my son, for he is an epileptic and he suffers terribly; for often he falls into the fire and often into the water. 16 And I brought him to your disciples, and they could not heal him." 17 And Jesus answered, "O faithless and perverse generation, how long am I to be with you? How long am I to bear with you? Bring him here to me." 18 And Jesus rebuked him, and the demons came out of him and the boy was cured instantly. 19 Then the disciples came to Jesus privately and said, "Why could we not cast it out?" 20 He said to them, "Because of your little faith. For truly, I say to you, if you have faith as a grain of mustard seed, you will say to this mountain, 'Move from here to there,' and it will move; and nothing will be impossible to you." 23 As they were gathering in Galilee, Jesus said to them, "The Son of man is to be delivered into the hands of men, and they will kill him, and he will be raised on the third day". And they were greatly distressed.

It appears the disciples were now established as a

team regularly sharing the work of delivering Christ's message and healing. It must have been a much more guaranteed option to approach the disciples as opposed to struggling with the crowd to get to Jesus, but they must have been successful to a degree in the healing they offered, otherwise no one would have bothered to come to them; but they obviously also had their failures.

Disciples arguing who should be greatest. Forbidding man to cast out demons

Mark 9. 33 – 41   (RSV)

33 And they came to Capernaum; and when they were in the house he asked them "What were you discussing on the way?" 34 But they were silent; for on the way they had discussed with one another who was the greatest. 35 And he sat down and called the twelve; and he said to them, "If any one would be first, he must be last of all and servant of all." And he took a child, and put him in the midst of them; and taking him in his arms, he said to them, 37 "Whoever receives one such child in my name receives me; and whoever receives me receives not me but him who sent me."

38   John said to him, "Teacher, we saw a man

casting out Demons in your name, and we forbade him, because he was not following us." 39 But Jesus said, "Do not forbid him; for no one who does a mighty work in my name will be able to soon after speak evil of me. 40 For he that is not against us is for us. 41 For truly, I say to you, whoever gives you a cup of water to drink because you bear the name of Christ, will by no means lose his reward.

It is interesting that Jesus does not look for any acknowledgement of him in respect of any good works. Wherever they are, and from whomever they come, they will be affirmation of the kingdom Jesus proclaims if they are genuine. If they are not, they will in due time be revealed as such. 'By their fruits you shall know them.'

How many times should I forgive my brother?

Matthew 18. 21 – 35   (RSV)
21 Then Peter came up and said to him, "Lord, how often shall my brother sin against me, and I forgive him? As many as seven times?" 22 Jesus said to him, "I do not say to you seven times, but seventy times seven.

23 "Therefore the kingdom of heaven may be

compared to a king who wished to settle accounts with his servants. 24 When he began the reckoning one was brought to him who owed him ten thousand talents; 25 and as he could not pay, his Lord ordered him to be sold, with his wife and children and all that he had, and payment to be made. 26 So the servant fell on his knees imploring him, 'Lord, have patience with me, and I will pay you everything.' 27 And out of pity for him the Lord of that servant released him and forgave him the debt. 28 But that same servant, as he went out, came upon one of his fellow servants who owed him a hundred denarii. And seizing him by the throat he said, "Pay what you owe." 29 So his fellow servant fell down and besought him, 'Have patience with me, and I will pay you.' 30 He refused and went and put him in prison till he should pay the debt. 31 When his fellow servants saw what had taken place, they were greatly distressed, and they went and reported to the Lord all that had taken place. 32 Then his Lord summoned him and said to him, "You wicked servant! I forgave you all that debt because you besought me; 33 and should not you have had mercy on your fellow servant, as I had mercy on you?' 34 And in anger his Lord delivered him to the jailers till he should pay all his debts. 35 So also my heavenly Father will do to everyone of you, if you do not forgive your brother from your heart."

Parable of the two prayers, Pharisee and tax collector

Luke 18. 9 – 14   (RSV)

9 He also told this parable to some who trusted in themselves that they were righteous and despised others: 10 "Two men went up into the temple to pray, one a Pharisee and the other a tax collector. 11   The Pharisee stood and prayed thus with himself, 'God, I thank thee that I am not like other men, extortioners, unjust, adulterers, or even like this tax collector. 12 I fast twice a week, I give tithes of all that I get.'   13 But the tax collector, standing far off, would not even lift up his eyes to heaven, but beat his breast, saying, 'God, be merciful to me a sinner!'   14 I tell you, this man went down to his house justified rather than the other; for every one who exalts himself will be humbled, but he who humbles himself will be exalted."

Let the children.come to me. Man asking what he should do. Camel through the eye of a needle

Mark 10. 13 – 31 (RSV)

13 And they were bringing children to him, that he

might touch them; and the disciples rebuked them. But when Jesus saw it he was indignant, and said to them, "Let the children come to me, do not hinder them; for to such belong the kingdom of God. 15 Truly, I say to you, whoever does not receive the kingdom of God like a child shall not enter it." 16 And he took them in his arms and blessed them, laying his hands upon them.

17 And as he was setting out on his journey, a man ran up and knelt before him, and asked him, "Good Teacher, what must I do to inherit eternal life?" 18 And Jesus said to him, "Why do you call me good? No one is good but God alone. 19 You know the commandments: 'Do not kill, do not commit adultery, do not steal, do not bear false witness, do not defraud, honour your father and mother'" 20 And he said to him, "Teacher, all these I have observed from my youth." 21 And Jesus looking upon him loved him and said to him, "You lack one thing; go, sell what you have, and give to the poor, and you will have treasure in heaven; and come, follow me." 22 At that saying his countenance fell, and he went away sorrowful; for he had great possessions.

23 And Jesus looked around and said to his disciples, "How hard it will be for those who have riches to enter the kingdom of God!" 24 And the disciples were amazed at his words. But Jesus said to them again, "Children, how hard it is to enter the

kingdom of God. 25 It is easier for a camel to go through the eye of a needle than for a rich man to enter the kingdom of God." 26 And they were exceedingly astonished, and said to him, "Then who can be saved?" 27 Jesus looked at them and said, "With men it is impossible, but not with God; for all things are possible with God." 28 Peter began to say to him, "Lo, we have left everything and followed you." 29 Jesus said, "Truly, I say to you there is no one who has left house or brothers or sisters or mother or father or children or lands for my sake and for the gospel, 30 who will not receive a hundredfold now in this time, houses and brothers and sisters and mothers and children and lands, with persecutions, and in the age to come eternal life. 31 But many that are first will be last, and the last first."

Jesus was obviously a magnet for little children, with their instinctive recognition of a person's essence. One can imagine the disciples officiously trying to impose some limits on the crowd trying to get access, and, in the context of the little children who had not yet learnt to be anything other than themselves, the first requirement, surely, for the Kingdom of Heaven, getting it spectacularly wrong, with Jesus' indignant rebuke coming down to us in the incomparable beauty of the King James Bible language' "Suffer little children to come unto me, and forbid them not, for of such is the Kingdom of

God". The 'eye of the needle' comment was another that used to haunt my boyhood. Did *any* soft spot for mammon automatically rule one out of any possibility of heaven? Such an absolute, uncompromising impossibility is presented.

Again, it seems to me, Jesus is ready to cheat with a loophole for those who really want it. He lays the foundation with "With men it is impossible, but not with God; for all things are possible with God". Then, I have no idea how much academic support there is for the idea, but I remember a sermon in which it was suggested that there was a gate into Jerusalem that was so narrow it was nicknamed 'The Eye of the Needle', into which you could certainly count on having difficulty in persuading your camel to put its nose. If such a gate existed Jesus would have known of it.

Seek and you will find, knock and it shall be opened to you.

Chapter XIII
Parable of the labourers hired

Matthew 20. 1 – 16 (RSV)

"For the kingdom of heaven is like a householder who went out early in the morning to hire labourers for his vineyard. 2 After agreeing with the labourers for a denarius a day, he sent them into his vineyard. 3 And going out about the third hour he saw others standing idle in the marketplace; 4 And to them he said, 'You go into the vineyard too, and whatever is right I will give you.' So they went. 5 Going out again about the sixth hour and the ninth hour, he did the same. 6 And about the eleventh hour he went out and found others standing; and he said to them, 'Why do you stand here idle all day?' 7 They said to him, 'Because no one has hired us.' He said to them, 'Go into the vineyard too.' 8 And when evening came, the owner of the vineyard said to his stewards, 'Call the labourers and pay them their wages, beginning with the last to the first.' And when those hired about the eleventh hour came, each of them received a denarius. 10 Now when the first came, they thought they would receive more; but each of them also received a denarius. 11 And on receiving it they grumbled at the householder, 12 saying, 'These last worked only one hour, and you have made them equal to us who have borne the burden of the day and the scorching heat.' 13 But he replied to one of them, 'Friend I am doing you no wrong; did you not agree with me for a denarius? 14 Take what belongs to you, and go; I choose to give to this last as I give to you. 15 Am I not allowed to do what I choose with what belongs to me? Or do you begrudge my generosity?' 16 So the last will be first, and the first last."

One can sympathise with the concept that recompense should be proportionate to effort put in, but when the reward is infinite love, this presents some difficulties.

Telling them what will happen to the Son of Man

Mark 9. 30 – 32, 10. 32 – 34 (RSV)
30 They went on from there and passed through Galilee. And he would not have anyone know it; 31 for he was teaching his disciples, saying to them, "The Son of man will be delivered into the hands of men, and they will kill him; and when he is killed,

after three days he will rise." 32 But they did not understand the saying, and they were afraid to ask him.

10. 32 And they were on the road, going up to Jerusalem, and Jesus was walking ahead of them; and they were amazed, and those who followed were afraid. And taking the twelve again, he began to tell them what was to happen to him 33 saying, "Behold we are going up to Jerusalem; and the Son of man will be delivered to the chief priests and the scribes, and they will condemn him to death, and deliver him to the Gentiles; 34 and they will mock him, and spit upon him, and scourge him, and kill him; and after three days he will rise.

You can understand the disciples' dismay and confusion. Here is the man who has apparently offered the answer to life, and in the process turned their own lives upside down; to follow whom they have given up everything, whom they believe to be the Messiah and the Son of God, suddenly talking about being killed in the near future, with the same incomprehensible reference to afterward rising in three days.

No one wants to ask him anything in case he repeats what he has just said. Perhaps if they don't say anything and just carry on, with all the excitement and activity of Passover it will somehow get swept aside and forgotten.

The mother of James and John

Matthew 20. 20 – 28   (RSV)

20 Then the mother of the sons of Zebedee came to him, with her sons, and kneeling before him she asked him for something. 21 And he said to her "What do you want?" She said to him "Command that these two sons of mine may sit, one at your right hand and one at your left, in your kingdom." 22 But Jesus answered, "You do not know what you are asking. Are you able to drink the cup that I am to drink?" They said to him, "We are able." 23 He said to them, "You will drink my cup, but to sit at my right hand and at my left is not mine to grant, but it is for those for whom it is being prepared by my Father." 24 And when the ten heard it, they were indignant at the two brothers. 25 But Jesus called them to him and said, "You know that the rulers of the Gentiles lord it over them and their great men exercise authority over them. 26 It shall not be so among you; but whoever would be great among you must be your servant, 27 and whoever would be first among you must be your slave; 28 even as the Son of man came not to be served but to serve and to give his life as a ransom for many."

Classic mother looking out for her sons, even if she unwittingly somewhat overreached herself in the position she was driving at for them. It is interesting, though, that the older generation appear to have also accepted that Jesus had some kind of kingdom in his gift.

You might have expected them to be less well disposed towards the man who had taken their children away from their family and marital duties, abandoning home, jobs, responsibilities, and who, in spite of all the reported wonders associated with him, was dependent on the charity of others to survive.

Jesus lances the boil of resentment from the other disciples and of all future jealousies with his statement of what greatness means in his kingdom. 'If you want to be great, be the most humble servant to all.'

Blind man healed on way to Jericho

Luke 18. 35 – 43 (RSV)

35 As he drew near to Jericho, a blind man was sitting by the roadside begging; 36 and hearing a multitude going by, he enquired what this meant. 37 They told him," Jesus of Nazareth is passing by." 38

And he cried, "Jesus, Son of David, have mercy on me!" 40 And those who were in front rebuked him, telling him to be silent; but he cried out all the more, "Son of David, have mercy on me!" 39 And Jesus stopped, and commanded him to be brought to him; and when he came near, he asked him, 41 "What do you want me to do for you?" He said, "Lord, let me receive my sight." 42 And Jesus said to him, "Receive your sight; your faith has made you well." 43 And immediately he received his sight and followed him, glorifying God; and all the people, when they saw it, gave praise to God.

It is striking how often Jesus checks with those calling for his help what it is they are looking for. To the sick man at the pool at Bethzatha – "Do you want to be healed?" And here, to the blind man – "What do you want me to do for you?"

Pretty obvious you might think; but perhaps not. If your heart's desire is an end to your fleshly suffering, then, through Jesus, in your knowledge of being completely surrounded by God's love, this could be brought about. But perhaps instead you might wish for a further opening of your heart to allow a closer union with God. Can you imagine the enablement that would come from Christ if he was to be asked for this?

Zacchaeus

Luke 19. 1 – 10   (RSV)

He entered Jericho and was passing through.   2
And there was a man named Zacchaeus; he was a
chief tax collector, and rich. 3 And he sought to see
who Jesus was, but could not, on account of the
crowd, because he was small of stature. 4 So he
ran on ahead and climbed up into a sycamore tree to
see him, for he was to pass that way. 5 And when
Jesus came to the place, he looked up and said to
him, "Zacchaeus, make haste and come down; for I
must stay at your house today." 6 So he made
haste and came down, and received him joyfully. 7
And when they saw it they all murmured, "He has
gone in to be the guest of a man who is a sinner." 8
And Zacchaeus stood and said to the Lord, "Behold,
Lord, the half of my goods I give to the poor; and if I
have defrauded any one of anything, I restore it
fourfold." 9 And Jesus said to him, "Today salvation
has come to this house, since he also is a son of
Abraham. 10 For the Son of man came to seek and
to save the lost."

Again, it's one of those little details that can simply
only be authentic; the little man up in the sycamore
tree with Jesus stopping to look up and talk to him.
Then, in the overwhelming love that came into his
house, Zacchaeus embracing the truth he has, until

then, always turned his eyes from.

Even his brothers...

John 7. 1 – 5 (RSV)
After this Jesus went about in Galilee; he would not
go about in Judea, because the Jews sought to kill
him. 2 Now the Jews' feast of Tabernacles was at
hand. 3 So his brothers said to him, "Leave here
and go to Judea that your disciples may see the
works you are doing. 4 For no man works in secret
if he seeks to be known openly. If you do these
things, show yourself to the world." 5 For even his
brothers did not believe in him.

You can hardly blame them, but it shows no wonder,
however great or well attested, will necessarily be
accepted as such.

Woman caught in adultery

John 8. 1 – 11 (RSV)
But Jesus went to the Mount of Olives. 2 Early in
the morning he came again to the temple; all the
people came to him, and he sat down and taught
them. 3 The scribes and the Pharisees brought a

woman who had been caught in adultery, and placing her in the midst   4   they said to him, "Teacher, this woman has been caught in the act of adultery. 5 Now in the law Moses commanded us to stone such. What do you say about her?" 6   This they said to test him, that they might have some charge to bring against him. Jesus bent down and wrote with his finger on the ground. 7   And as they continued to ask him, he stood up and said to them, "Let him who is without sin among you be the first to throw a stone at her."   8 And again he bent down and wrote with his finger on the ground. 9 But when they heard it, they went away, one by one, beginning with the eldest, and Jesus was left alone with the woman standing before him.   10   Jesus looked up and said to her, "Woman, where are they? Has no one condemned you? 11 She said, "No one, Lord." And Jesus said, "Neither do I condemn you; go and do not sin again."

Again, the attempt by the Temple rulers to entangle Jesus in controversy. They suspect he will not favour the barbaric law of stoning an adulteress. The woman's guilt is apparently not in question.

If he opposes its execution he is directly opposing a dictum of Moses, making himself liable to all sorts of charges. If he supports it he has given the go-ahead and aligned himself with a savage punishment, in the process conceding from the faith he proclaims some degree of subservience to the Temple authorities and the letter of the law.

I love the image of Jesus staying silent, bending down and writing with his finger on the ground. What was going through his mind? "I've got to answer this, but how?" They must have thought they'd got him. Then he stands up and with one devastating sentence simply transfers it all back into human terms. "Let him who is without sin be the first to throw a stone at her." One by one they slink away, the eldest being the first to recognise the impossibility of the challenge.

Chapter XIV
Man blind from birth

John 9. 1 – 41 (RSV)

As he passed by, he saw a man blind from his birth. 2 And his disciples asked him, "Rabbi, who sinned, this man or his parents, that he was born blind?" 3 Jesus answered, "It was not that this man sinned, or his parents, but that the works of God might be made manifest in him. 4 We must work the works of him who sent me, while it is day; night comes, when no one can work. 5 As long as I am in the world, I am the light of the world." 6 As he said this, he spat on the ground and made clay of the spittle and anointed the man's eyes with the clay, saying to him, "Go wash in the pool of Siloam (which means Sent). So he went and washed and came back seeing. 8 The neighbours and those who had seen him before as a beggar', said, "Is not this the man who used to sit and beg?" 9 Some said, "It is he"; others said, "No, but he is like him." He said, "I am the man." 10 They said to him, "Then how were your eyes opened?" 11 He answered,"The man called Jesus made clay and anointed my eyes and said to me, 'Go to Siloam and wash'; so I went and washed and received my sight. 12 They said to him, "Where is he? He said, "I do not know'" 13 They brought to the Pharisees the man who had formerly been blind. 14 Now it was a sabbath day when Jesus made the clay and opened his eyes. 15 The Pharisees again asked him how he had received his sight and he said to them, "He put clay on my eyes, and I washed, and I see." 16 Some of the Pharisees said, "This man is not from God, for he does not keep the sabbath." But others said, "How can a man who is a sinner do such signs?" There was a division among them. 17 So they again said to the blind man, "What do you say about him, since he has opened your eyes?" He said, "He is a prophet."

18 The Jews did not believe that he had been blind and had received his sight, until they called the parents of the man who had received his sight, 19 and asked them, "Is this your son, who you say was born blind? How then does he now see?" 20 His parents answered, "We know that this is our son, and that he was born blind; 21 but how he now sees we do not know, nor do we know who opened his eyes. Ask him; he is of age, he will speak for himself." 22 His parents said this because they feared the Jews, for the Jews had already agreed that if any one should confess him to be Christ, he was to be put out of the synagogue. 23 Therefore his parents said, "He is of age, ask him."

24 So for the second time they called the man

who had been blind, and said to him, "Give God the praise; we know that this man is a sinner." 25 He answered, "Whether he is a sinner, I do not know; one thing I know that though I was blind, now I see." 26 They said to him, "What did he do to you? How did he open your eyes?" 27 He answered them, "I have told you already, and you would not listen. Why do you want to hear it again? Do you too want to become his disciples?" 28 And they reviled him, saying, "You are his disciple, but we are disciples of Moses. 29 We know that God has spoken to Moses, but as for this man, we do not know where he comes from." 30 The man answered, "Why this is a marvel! You do not know where he comes from, and yet he opened my eyes. 31 We know that God does not listen to sinners, but if anyone is a worshipper of God and does his will, God listens to him. 32 Never since the world began has it been heard that any one opened the eyes of a man born blind. 33 If this man were not from God, he could do nothing." 34 They answered him, "You were born in utter sin, and would you teach us?" And they cast him out.

35 Jesus heard that they had cast him out, and having found him he said, "Do you believe in the Son of man?" 36 He answered "And who is he, sir, that I may believe in him?" 37 Jesus said to him, "You have seen him, and it is he who speaks to you. 38 He said, "Lord, I believe"; and he worshipped him.

163

39 Jesus said, "For judgement I came into this world, that those who do not see may see, and that those who see may become blind." 40 Some of the Pharisees near him heard this, and they said to him, "Are we also blind?" 41 Jesus said to them, "If you were blind, you would have no guilt; but now that you say 'We see,' your guilt remains.

I think the reason I like this story so much is that this is how I would like to have behaved to Jesus' touch. He is so wonderfully forthright, the blind man.

"Well this is just marvellous isn't it! Here's the man who's done something nobody's ever done in the world before, giving me my sight who was blind, and you're not sure of whether he comes from God or not!"

I hope I would have been so true, but I worry that I would have been much more like his parents, terrified of getting on the wrong side of the Temple authorities.

"Well yes, I was blind, but don't ask me how I can see now. It's not my fault what happened. He just did it to me."

Jesus good shepherd

John 10. 1 – 18   (RSV)
"Truly, truly, I say to you, he who does not enter the

sheepfold by the door but climbs in by another way, that man is a thief and a robber; 2 but he who enters by the door is the shepherd of the sheep. 3 To him the gatekeeper opens; the sheep hear his voice, and he calls his own sheep by name and leads them out. 4 When he has brought out all his own, he goes before them, and the sheep follow him, for they know his voice. 5 A stranger they will not follow, but they will flee from him, for they do not know the voice of strangers." 6 This figure Jesus used with them, but they did not understand what he was saying to them.

7 So Jesus again said to them, "Truly, truly, I say to you, I am the door of the sheep. 8 All who came before me are thieves and robbers; but the sheep did not heed them. 9 I am the door; if any one enters by me, he will be saved, and will go in and out and find pasture. 10 The thief comes only to steal and kill and destroy; I came that they may have life and have it abundantly. 11 I am the good shepherd. The good shepherd lays down his life for the sheep. 12 He who is a hireling and not a shepherd, whose own the sheep are not, sees the wolf coming and leaves the sheep and flees; and the wolf snatches them and scatters them. 13 He flees because he is a hireling and cares nothing for the sheep. 14 I am the good shepherd; I know my own and my own know me, 15 as the Father knows me and I know the Father; and I lay down my life for the sheep. 16

And I have other sheep, that are not of this fold; I must bring them also, and they will heed my voice. So there shall be one flock, one shepherd. 17 For this reason the Father loves me, because I lay down my life, that I may take it again. 18 No one takes it from me, but I lay it down of my own accord. I have power to lay it down, and I have power to take it again; this charge I have received from my Father."

Lazarus

John 11. 1 – 57   (RSV)

Now a certain man was ill, Lazarus of Bethany, the village of Mary and her sister Martha. 2 It was Mary who anointed the Lord with ointment and wiped his feet with her hair, whose brother Lazarus was ill. 3 So the sisters sent to him, saying, "Lord, he whom you love is ill." 4 But when Jesus heard it, he said, "This illness is not unto death; it is for the glory of God, so that the Son of God may be glorified by means of it."

5 Now Jesus loved Martha and her sister and Lazarus. 6 So when he heard that he was ill, he stayed two days longer in the place where he was. 7 Then after this he said to the disciples, "Let us go into Judea again." 8 The disciples said to him, "Rabbi, the Jews were but now seeking to stone you, and are you going there again?" 9 Jesus answered,

"Are there not twelve hours in the day? If any one walks in the day, he does not stumble, because he sees the light of this world. 10 But if any one walks in the night, he stumbles, because the light is not in him." 11 Thus he spoke, and then he said to them, "Our friend Lazarus has fallen asleep, but I go to awake him out of sleep." 12 The disciples said to him, "Lord, if he has fallen asleep, he will recover." 13 Now Jesus had spoken of his death, but they thought that he meant taking rest in sleep. 14 Then Jesus told them plainly, "Lazarus is dead; 15 and for your sake I am glad that I was not there, so that you may believe. But let us go to him" 16 Thomas, called the Twin said to his fellow disciples, "Let us also go, that we may die with him."

17   Now when Jesus came, he found that Lazarus had already been in the tomb four days. 18 Bethany was near Jerusalem about two miles off, 19 and many of the Jews had come to Martha and Mary to console them concerning their brother. 20 When Martha heard that Jesus was coming, she went and met him, while Mary sat in the house. 21 Martha said to Jesus, "Lord, if you had been here, my brother would not have died. 22 And even now I know that whatever you ask from God, God will give you." 23 Jesus said to her, "Your brother will rise again." 24 Martha said to him, "I know that he will rise again in the resurrection at the last day." 25 Jesus said to her, "I am the resurrection and the life;

he who believes in me, though he die, yet shall he live, 26 and whoever lives and believes in me shall never die. Do you believe this?" 27 She said to him, "Yes, Lord; I believe that you are the Christ, the Son of God, he who is coming into this world."

28 When she had said this, she went and called her sister Mary, saying quietly, "The Teacher is here and is calling for you." 29 And when she heard it she rose quickly and went to him. 30 Now Jesus had not yet come to the village, but was still in the place where Martha had met him. 31 When the Jews who were with her in the house, consoling her, saw Mary rise quickly and go out, they followed her, supposing that she was going to the tomb to weep there. 32 Then Mary, when she came where Jesus was and saw him, fell at his feet, saying to him, "Lord, if you had been here, my brother would not have died." 33 When Jesus saw her weeping, and the Jews who came with her also weeping, he was deeply moved in spirit and troubled; 34 and he said, "Where have you laid him?" They said to him, "Lord, come and see." 35 Jesus wept. 35 So the Jews said, "See how he loved him!" 37 But some of them said, "Could not he who opened the eyes of the blind man have kept this man from dying?"

38 Then Jesus, deeply moved again, came to the tomb; it was a cave, and a stone lay upon it. 39 Jesus said, "Take away the stone." Martha, the sister of the dead man, said to him, "Lord, by this time

there will be an odor, for he has been dead four days." 40 Jesus said to her, "Did I not tell you that if you would believe you would see the glory of God?" 41 So they took away the stone. And Jesus lifted up his eyes and said, "Father, I thank thee that thou hast heard me. 42 I knew that thou hearest me always, but I have said this on account of the people standing by, that they may believe that thou didst send me." 43 When he had said this, he cried with a loud voice, "Lazarus come out." 44 The dead man came out, his hands and feet bound with bandages, and his face wrapped with a cloth. Jesus said to them, "Unbind him, and let him go."

45 Many of the Jews therefore, who had come with Mary and had seen what he did, believed in him; 46 but some of them went to the Pharisees and told them what Jesus had done. 47 So the chief priests and the Pharisees gathered the council, and said, "What are we to do? For this man performs many signs. 48 If we let him go on thus, every one will believe in him, and the Romans will come and destroy both our holy place and our nation." 49 But one of them, Caiaphas, who was high priest that year, said to them, "You know nothing at all; 50 you do not understand that it is expedient for you that one man should die for the people, and that the whole nation should not perish." 51 He did not say this of his own accord, but being high priest that year he prophesied that Jesus should die for the nation,

52 and not for the nation only, but to gather into one the children of God who are scattered abroad. 53 So from that day on they took counsel how to put him to death.

54 Jesus therefore no longer went about openly among the Jews, but went from there to the country near the wilderness, to a town called Ephraim; and there he stayed with the disciples.

55 Now the Passover of the Jews was at hand, and many went up from the country to Jerusalem before the Passover, to purify themselves. 56 They were looking for Jesus and saying to one another as they stood in the temple, "What do you think? That he will not come to the feast?" 57 Now the chief priests and the Pharisees had given orders that if any one knew where he was, he should let them know, so that they might arrest him.

My position is as always on miracles. This one, though, is the one I find I have the most difficulty with. The account is completely uncompromising. Martha, speaking of her certainty that if Jesus had been there her brother would not have died says "And even now I know that whatever you ask from God, God will give you." Jesus has apparently stayed away until he is certain that Lazarus will be dead. And he simply comes to the tomb and calls to him to come out.

The report is enough to throw the scribes and

Pharisees into panic. If indeed this act is confirmed they may as well leave the Temple. Their time will be up. One can't help feeling that their reference to the dangers of the Roman reaction is an excuse for them to continue their opposition to Jesus. Caiaphas translates this feeling into a firm resolve to make Jesus a sacrifice 'for the whole nation'.

I found John's comment on Caiaphas's statement very confusing. It almost sounded to me as if he was acting as an apologist for him.

'He did not say this of his own accord, but being high priest that year he prophesied that Jesus should die for the nation and not for the nation only, but to gather into one the children of God who are scattered abroad.'

My spiritual confidant, guide, and friend Rev Harold Stringer offers another possibility. He suggests that John never fails to grasp an opportunity to slip in a little promotion of the faith alongside his reporting of the facts. With the benefit of hindsight, therefore, he makes Caiaphas – through his statement that it was "expedient for you that one man (Jesus) should die for the people" – the unwitting and unintended prophesier ("he did not say this of his own accord") of the exact opposite of what he desired – that the nation and beyond would indeed be saved by Jesus' sacrifice, but not, as Caiaphas imagined, through the elimination of his teaching, but rather, stemming from his death, through the world-wide dissemination of the faith he has proclaimed.

In the meantime this story remains, for me, a challenge, and I presume will continue to do so.

Chapter XV
Entry to Jerusalem.
Palms

Matthew 21. 1 – 11   (RSV)

And when they drew near to Jerusalem and came to Bethphage, to the Mount of Olives, then Jesus sent two disciples, 2 saying to them, "Go into the village opposite you, and immediately you will find an ass, and a colt with her; untie them and bring them to me. 3 If any one says anything to you, you shall say, 'The Lord has need of them,' and he will send them immediately." 4 This took place to fulfil what was spoken by the prophet, saying,

> 5 "Tell the daughter of Zion,
> Behold, your king is coming to you,
> humble, and mounted on an ass, and on a colt, the foal of an ass."

6   The disciples went, and did as Jesus had directed them; 7 they brought the ass and the colt, and put their garments on them, and he sat on them. 8 Most of the crowd spread their garments on the road, and others cut branches from trees and spread them on the road. 9   And the crowds that went before him and that followed him shouted, "Hosanna

to the son of David! Blessed is he who comes in the name of the Lord! Hosanna in the highest!" 10 And when he entered Jerusalem, all the city was stirred, saying, "Who is this?" 11 And the crowd said, "This is the prophet Jesus from Nazareth of Galilee."

My favourite theory about the mysterious ass and colt made ready for Jesus is based on the proposition that Judas was a member of the Zealots, the extremist sect with the avowed intention of freeing the Jews from Roman rule.

The Zealots were looking for the coming of the Messiah, so fervently believed in by the Jews, who would restore the chosen people to their former greatness – in their terms by leading the armed insurrection they devoted their energies to preparing for. Jesus presented them with something of a problem. He clearly fitted the bill as Messiah with the unceasing and extraordinary teaching and wonders of his mission on every side, and was accepted by many as such already. The only trouble was his teaching was exclusively spiritual and moral. There was no reference to any kind of nationalistic or patriotic aims or ambitions.

The Messiah was the trump card the Zealots were only waiting for to set off the revolution. It would be a disaster if the wrong person came to be identified as he. With Jesus' knowledge, then, Judas would have been planted in the disciples to observe what was developing and report back to his bosses.

In this issue, the interests of the Zealots and those of the Temple came together. Jesus' call for a purging of the Temple teaching and return to the real spiritual values that had formed the foundation of the Jewish faith threatened to drastically undermine the authority of the Scribes and Pharisees, exposing the long-standing abuses they applied in ritual and procedure to increase their power and income.

For them, too, it would be a complete disaster if Jesus came to be generally recognised as the Messiah. Jesus' immense popularity and the huge crowds that followed him everywhere meant they could not do in a public place what they would have liked to do – arrest him and come up with charges of blasphemy. They would probably have been lynched if they had tried. They needed to find somewhere where he was on his own, but how, where?

According to the theory that I favour, as Passover approached, the Zealots, through Judas, gave Jesus one more chance. Going up to Passover he was to make clear to them, once and for all, his intentions. They would have an ass and a colt waiting for him at a point outside Jerusalem. If he rode into Jerusalem on the colt it would mean he was ready to lead the armed revolt. If he chose the ass it would mean his ministry would continue as a strictly spiritual mission.

Choosing the ass, Jesus would have been very well

aware of the implications, and the agent, Judas, through whom they would be precipitated.

Once they had their answer, the Zealots, too, had a problem of how to get rid of Jesus. They also had to beware of the crowd. They did not wish to risk the unpopularity of having his death attributed to their name. The solution to both their and the Temple authorities' problem lay in each other. The Zealots, through Judas, had only to tip off the Temple authorities where Jesus was to be found alone, and leave the rest to them.

The colt is referred to as the foal of the ass, so perhaps it would not make sense for Jesus to have ridden it, but it adds up for me that some pre-arranged signal was given by Jesus in the way he used the two animals left for him.

Overturning the money tables

Matthew 21. 12 – 17   (RSV)

12 And Jesus entered the temple of God and drove out all who sold and bought in the temple, and he overturned the tables of the money-changers and the seats of those who sold pigeons. 12 He said to them, "It is written, 'My house shall be called a house of prayer'; but you make it a den of robbers."

14 And the blind and lame came to him in the

temple, and he healed them. 15 But when the chief priests and the scribes saw the wonderful things that he did, and the children crying out in the temple, "Hosanna to the Son of David!" They were indignant; 16 and they said to him, "Do you hear what they are saying?" And Jesus said to them, "Yes; have you never read

     'Out of the mouth of babes and
        sucklings
     thou hast wrought perfect praise'?"

17 And leaving them, he went out of the city to Bethany and lodged there.

Jesus was a threat, really, to every form of establishment.

Bethany: home of Lazarus, Mary, and Martha, and of Simon the Leper.

By what authority?

Matthew 21. 23 – 27   (RSV)
23   And when he entered the temple, the chief priests and the elders of the people came up to him as he was teaching, and said, "By what authority are you doing these things, and who gave you this authority?" 24 Jesus answered them, "I also will ask you a question; and if you tell me the answer, then I also will tell you by what authority I do these things.

25   The baptism of John, whence was it? From heaven or from men?" And they argued with one another, "If we say, 'From heaven,' he will say to us 'Why then did you not believe him?' But if we say, 'From men,' we are afraid of the multitude; for all hold that John was a prophet."   27   So they answered Jesus, "We do not know." And he said to them, "Neither will I tell you by what authority I do these things.

If they can only just get him to declare the already obvious, that the source of his works is God, they will have him. He will in a moment be in a religious court charged with blasphemy.

But they never seem able to pin him down. 'Yes', he will oblige them with an answer on the source of his power, if they will first answer the unanswerable. And so he eludes them again.

Killing the messengers

Matthew 21. 33 – 45   (RSV)
33 "Hear another parable. There was a householder who planted a vineyard, and set a hedge around it, and dug a wine press in it, and built a tower, and let it out to tenants, and went into another country. 34 When the season of fruit drew near, he sent his

servants to the tenants to get his fruit; 35 and the tenants took his servants and beat one, killed another, and stoned another. 36 Again he sent other servants, more than the first; and they did the same to them. 37 Afterward he sent his son to them, saying, "They will respect my son.' 38 But when the tenants saw the son, they said to themselves, 'This is the heir; come, let us kill him and have his inheritance.' 39 And they took him and cast him out the vineyard, and killed him. 40 When therefore the owner of the vineyard comes what will he do to those tenants?" 41 They said to him, "He will put those wretches to a miserable death, and let out the vineyard to other tenants who will give him the fruits in their seasons"

42 Jesus said to them, "Have you never read in the scriptures:

'The very stone which the builders rejected

has become the head of the corner;

this was the Lord's doing,

and it is marvellous in our eyes'?

43 Therefore I tell you, the kingdom of God will be taken away from you and given to a nation producing the fruit of it."

45 When the chief priests and the Pharisees heard his parable they perceived that he was speaking about them. 46 But when they tried to arrest him, they feared the multitude, because they held him to be a prophet.

Parable of the banquet

Matthew 22. 1 – 14   (RSV)

And again Jesus spoke to them in parables, saying 2 "The kingdom of heaven may be compared to a king who gave a marriage feast for his son, 3 and sent his servants to call those who were invited to the marriage feast; but they would not come.   4 Again he sent other servants, saying, 'Tell those who are invited, Behold, I have made ready my dinner, my oxen and my fat calves are killed, and everything is ready; come to the marriage feast.' 5 But they made light of it and went off, one to his farm, another to his business, 6 while the rest seized his servants, treated them shamefully, and killed them.   7 The king was angry, and he sent his troops and destroyed those murderers and burned their city. 8 then he said to his servants, 'The wedding is ready, but those invited were not worthy. 9 Go therefore to the thoroughfares, and invite to the marriage feast as many as you find.' 10 And those servants went out into the streets and gathered all whom they found, both bad and good; so the wedding hall was filled with guests.

11 "But when the King came in to look at the guests, he saw there a man who had no wedding garment; 12 and he said to him, 'Friend, how did you get in here without a wedding garment?' And he was speechless.   13   Then the king said to the

attendants, 2 Bind him hand and foot, and cast him into the outer darkness; there men will weep and gnash their teeth.' 14 For many are called, but few are chosen."

I had always had the greatest difficulty getting my head round what was meant here until I heard Rev Dr Sam Wells' sermon on the topic which I found marvellously illuminating.

The banquet itself is about the feast of love available in God's presence. It is a wedding banquet about the union of God and humanity for which humanity was created.

The invitation to the banquet is just that – the promptings of our own hearts, the example of others, the call of the prophets. The main feature of the response is negative. The banquet may be a good idea but usually it intrudes too much onto our own plans. We may simply not have time to even consider it, or to some its very concept may be perceived to pose a threat to the position they have created for themselves.

Initially the invitation went to the Jews for reasons theorised over earlier. Now, instead of coming through them it comes direct to the rest of us. The invitation is to everyone, good and bad; the only requirement is, if you intend to accept, that you take seriously the wonder of the love you are offered and prepare a little to be able to engage with it and offer a little back. This is the appropriate wedding garment referred to. If you make no preparation and simply turn up, you will feel like a fish out of water.

There are three questions Sam says we need to ask ourselves.

Do we believe the world was created so that we might share in a banquet and be God's companions for ever?

Do we believe that through Jesus and at great cost the invitation to that banquet was extended to us and many others by amazing grace?

Do we believe that the way to answer God's invitation is to allow the Holy Spirit to fashion our lives so that when we are called to the banquet we clearly belong there because we've been living the life of the banquet and sharing the company of those invited to the banquet long before we were finally a guest there?

Sam suggests it could be that those three questions are the most important ones anyone will ever ask us.

Chapter XVI
Is it lawful to pay Caesar?

Matthew 22. 15 – 22   (RSV)

15 Then the Pharisees went and took counsel how to entangle him in his talk. 16 And they sent their disciples to him along with the Herodians, saying, "Teacher, we know that you are true, and teach the way of God truthfully, and care for no man; for you do not regard the position of men. 17 Tell us, then, what you think. Is it lawful to pay taxes to Caesar, or not?" 18 But Jesus, aware of their malice, said, "Why put me to the test, you hypocrites? 19 Show me the money for the tax." 20 And they brought him a coin. 20 And Jesus said to them, "Whose likeness and inscription is this?" 21 They said, "Caesar's." Then he said to them ,"Render therefore to Caesar the things that are Caesar's, and to God the things that are God's". 22 When they heard it, they marvelled: and they left him and went away.

It must have been so disappointing for Jesus that never did the Scribes and Pharisees attempt to engage with the challenge and content of his mission; always just looking to see if his words could be twisted into the committing of some ritualistic or legalistic blunder.

On paper it was the perfect trap question, dragging in the unresolved issue of the compatibility of Jewish religious and Roman secular law as well as the deeply resented requirement to pay Roman taxes. 'No' and there was instant serious trouble with the Roman authorities. 'Yes' and Jesus would have been presented as choosing submission to the laws of the occupying power as preferred to the requirements of his own religion, as well as toadying to the Romans in exhorting payment of their hated taxes.

And then the perfect response, blowing the perfect question to nowhere and leaving his opponents literally gasping to each other in admiration.

Which is the greatest commandment?

Mark 12. 28 – 34 (RSV)

28 And one of the scribes came up and heard them disputing with one another, and seeing that he answered them well, asked him, "Which commandment is the first of all?" 29 Jesus answered, "The first is, 'Hear, O Israel: the Lord our

God, the Lord is one; 30 and you shall love the Lord your God with all your heart, and with all your soul, and with all your mind, and with all your strength. 31 The second is this, 'You shall love your neighbour as yourself. There is no other commandment greater than these. 32 And the scribe said to him, "You have truly said that he is one and there is no other but he, 33 and to love him with all the heart, and with all the understanding, and with all the strength, and to love one's neighbour as oneself, is much more that all whole burnt offerings and sacrifices" 34 And when Jesus saw that he answered wisely he said to him, "You are not far from the kingdom of God." And after that no one dared to ask him any question.

The widow's mite

Mark 12. 41 – 44 (RSV)

41 And he sat down opposite the treasury, and watched the multitude putting money into the treasury. Many rich people put in large sums. 42 And a poor widow came, and put in two copper coins, which make a penny. 43 And he called his disciples to him, and said to them, "Truly, I say to you, this poor widow has put in more than all those who are contributing to the treasury. 44 For they all contributed out of their abundance; but she out of

her poverty has put in everything she had, her whole living."

The foolish virgins and the parable of the talents

Matthew 25. 1 – 30 (RSV)

"Then the kingdom of heaven shall be compared to ten maidens who took their lamps and went to meet the bridegroom. 2 Five of them were foolish, and five were wise. 3 For when the foolish took their lamps, they took no oil with them; 4 but the wise took flasks of oil with their lamps. 5 As the bridegroom was delayed, they all slumbered and slept. 6 But at midnight there was a cry, 'Behold, the bridegroom! Come out to meet him.' 7 Then all those maidens rose and trimmed their lamps. 8 And the foolish said to the wise, 'Give us some of your oil, for our lamps are going out.' 9 But the wise replied, 'Perhaps there will not be enough for us and for you; go rather to the dealers and buy for yourselves.' 10 And while they went to buy, the bridegroom came, and those who were ready went in with him to the marriage feast; and the door was shut. 11 Afterward the other maidens came also, saying, 'Lord, Lord, open to us.' 12 But he replied, 'Truly, I say to you, I do not know you.' 13 Watch therefore, for you know neither the day nor the hour.

14 "For it will be as when a man going on a journey called his servants and entrusted to them his property; 15 To one he gave five talents, to another two, to another one, to each according to his ability. Then he went away. 16 He who had received the five talents went at once and traded with them; and he made five talents more. 17 So also, he who had two talents made two talents more. 18 But he who had received the one talent went and dug in the ground and hid his master's money. 19 Now after a long time the master of those servants came and settled accounts with them. 20 And he who had received the five talents came forward, bringing five talents more, saying. "Master, you delivered to me five talents; here I have made five talents more.' 21 His master said to him, "Well done, good and faithful servant; you have been faithful over a little, I will set you over much; enter into the joy of your master.' 22 And he also who had the two talents came forward, saying, "Master you delivered to me two talents; here I have made two talents more.' 23 His master said to him, "Well done, good and faithful servant; you have been faithful over a little, I will set you over much; enter into the joy of your master.' 24 He also who had received the one talent came forward, saying, "Master, I knew you to be a hard man, reaping where you did not sow and gathering where you did not winnow; 25 so I was afraid, and I went

and hid your talent in the ground. Here you have what is yours.' 26 But his master answered him, "You wicked and slothful servant! You knew that I reap where I have not sowed, and gather where I have not winnowed? 27 Then you ought to have invested my money with the bankers, and at my coming I should have received what was my own with interest. 28 So take the talent from him, and give it to him who has ten talents. 29 For to everyone who has will more be given, and he will have abundance; but from him who has not, even what he has will be taken away. 30 And cast the worthless servant into the outer darkness; there men will weep and gnash their teeth.'

This seems another bit of a hard story with the wise virgins behaving, you might say, in a rather un-Christian-like way. Perhaps one should think of it as the contrast between someone who has regularly given time to the development of their spiritual life and understanding, and someone who has not. When their lives come to an end, however much she might like to, the 'wise' one simply cannot just transfer any of the 'spiritual readiness' she has gained to the 'foolish' one.

In his reporting of the parable of the talents, *Luke* starts with a preamble to it to try to think through what was in Jesus' mind when he told it – "As they heard these things he proceeded to tell them a parable because he was near Jerusalem and because they supposed that the Kingdom of God was to appear immediately" - so as to alert them, on thinking back, that, his having 'gone on a journey', in the event that the Kingdom of Heaven did not, of its own volition, immediately appear, it was their duty in the meanwhile to use the talents they had been given in his service.

As regards the talents themselves, we, most of us, surely, feel a twinge of insecurity? One and a half talents might be the best we could hope to gather together. We would hope indeed not to be one who has simply not found time at all to make use of and develop any of the gifts with which they were endowed.

The sheep and the goats

Matthew 25. 31 – 46   (RSV)
31 "When the Son of man comes in his glory, and all the angels with him, then he will sit on his glorious throne.   32   Before him will be gathered all the nations, and he will separate them one from another as a Shepherd separates the sheep from the goats, 33 and he will place the sheep at his right hand, but the goats at the left.   34   Then the king will say to those at his right hand, 'Come, O blessed of my father, inherit the kingdom prepared for you from the

foundation of the world; 35 for I was hungry and you gave me food, I was thirsty and you gave me drink, I was a stranger and you welcomed me, 36 I was naked and you clothed me, I was sick and you visited me, I was in prison and you came to me.' 37 Then the righteous will answer him, 'Lord when did we see thee hungry and feed thee, or thirsty and give thee drink? 38 And when did we see thee a stranger and welcome thee or naked and clothe thee? 39 And when did we see thee sick or in prison and visit thee?' 40 And the King will answer them, 'Truly, I say to you, as you did it to one of the least of these my brethren, you did it to me.' 41 Then he will say to those at his left hand, 'Depart from me, you cursed, into the eternal fire prepared for the devil and his angels; 42 for I was hungry and you gave me no food, I was thirsty and you gave me no drink, 43 I was a stranger and you did not welcome me, naked and you did not clothe me, sick and in prison and you did not visit me.' 44 Then they also will answer, 'Lord, when did we see thee hungry or thirsty or a stranger or naked or sick or in prison, and did not minister to thee?' 45 Then he will answer them, 'Truly I say to you, as you did it not to one of the least of these, you did it not to me.' 46 And they will go away into eternal punishment, but the righteous into eternal life."

Chief priests and elders looking how to arrest Jesus

Matthew 26. 1- 5 (RSV)

When Jesus had finished all these sayings, he said to his disciples, 2 "You know that after two days the Passover is coming, and the Son of Man will be delivered up to be crucified."

3 Then the chief priests and the elders of the people gathered in the palace of the high priest, who was called Caiaphas, 4 and took counsel together in order to arrest Jesus by stealth and kill him. 5 But they said, "Not during the feast, lest there be a tumult among the people."

Chapter XVII
Judas Iscariot. The Last Supper. The Cross

Matthew 26. 14 – 19   (RSV)

14 Then one of the twelve, who was called Judas Iscariot, went to the chief priests 15 and said, "What will you give me if I deliver him to you?" And they paid him thirty pieces of silver. 16 And from that moment he sought an opportunity to betray him.

17 Now on the first day of Unleavened Bread the disciples came to Jesus, saying, "Where will you have us prepare for you to eat the Passover?" 18 He said, "Go into the city to a certain one, and say to him, 'The teacher says, My time is at hand; I will keep the Passover at your house with my disciples'." 19 And the disciples did as Jesus had directed them, and they prepared the Passover.

John 13. 1 – 16. 33 (RSV)

Now before the feast of the Passover, when Jesus knew that his hour had come to depart out of this world to the Father, having loved his own who were in the world, he loved them to the end. 2 And during supper, when the devil had already put it into the heart of Judas Iscariot, Simon's son, to betray him, 3 Jesus, knowing that the Father had given all things into his hands, and that he had come from God and was going to God, 4 rose from supper, laid aside his garments, and girded himself with a towel. 5 Then he poured water into a basin, and began to wash the disciples feet, and to wipe them with the towel with which he was girded. 6 He came to Simon Peter; and Peter said to him, "Lord, do you wash my feet?" 7 Jesus answered him, "What I am doing you do not know now, but afterward you will understand." 8 Peter said to him, "You shall never wash my feet." Jesus answered him, "If I do not wash you, you have no part in me." 9 Simon Peter said to him, "Lord, not my feet only but also my hands and my head!" 10 Jesus said to him, "He who has bathed does not need to wash, except for his feet, but he is clean all over; and you are clean, but not every one of you." 11 For he knew who was to betray him; that was why he said, "You are not all clean."

12 When he had washed their feet, and taken his garments, and resumed his place, he said to them, "Do you know what I have done to you? 13 You call me Teacher and Lord; and you are right, for so I am. 14 If I then, your Lord and Teacher, have washed your feet, you also ought to wash one another's feet. 15 For I have given you an example, that you also should do as I have done to you. 16 Truly, truly, I

say to you, a servant is not greater than his master; nor is he who is sent greater than he who sent him. 17 If you know these things, blessed are you if you do them. 18 I am not speaking of you all; I know whom I have chosen; it is that the scripture may be fulfilled, 'He who ate my bread has lifted his heel against me.' 19 I tell you this now before it takes place, then when it does take place you may believe that I am he. 20 Truly, truly, I say to you, he who receives any one whom I send receives me; and he who receives me receives him who sent me."

21 When Jesus had thus spoken, he was troubled in spirit, and testified, "Truly, truly, I say to you, one of you will betray me." 22 The disciples looked at one another, uncertain of whom he spoke. 23 One of his disciples, whom Jesus loved, was lying close to the breast of Jesus; 24 so Simon Peter beckoned to him and said, "Tell us whom it is of whom he speaks." 25 So lying thus, close to the breast of Jesus, he said to him, "Lord, who is it?" Jesus answered, "It is he to whom I shall give this morsel when I have dipped it." So when he had dipped the morsel, he gave it to Judas, the son of Simon Iscariot.. 27 Then after the morsel, Satan entered into him. Jesus said to him, "What you are going to do, do quickly." 28 Now no one at the table knew why he said this to him. 29 Some thought that, because Judas had the money box, Jesus was telling him, "Buy what we need for the feast"; or, that

he should give something to the poor. 30 So, after receiving the morsel, he immediately went out; and it was night.

31 When he had gone out, Jesus said "Now is the Son of man glorified, and in him God is glorified; 32 if God is glorified in him, God will also glorify him in himself, and glorify him at once. 33 Little children, yet a little while I am with you. You will seek me; and as I said to the Jews so now I say to you, 'Where I am going you cannot come.' 34 A new commandment I give to you, that you love one another; even as I have loved you, that you also love one another. 35 By this all men will know that you are my disciples, if you have love for one another."

36 Simon Peter said to him, "Lord, where are you going?" Jesus answered, "Where I am going you cannot follow me now; but you shall follow afterward." 37 Peter said to him, "Lord why cannot I follow you now? I will lay down my life for you." 38 Jesus answered, "Will you lay down your life for me? Truly, truly, I say to you, the cock will not crow till you have denied me three times.

14. "Let not your hearts be troubled; believe in God, believe also in me. 2 In my Father's house are many rooms; if it were not so, would I have told you that I go to prepare a place for you? 3 And when I go and prepare a place for you, I will come again and will take you to myself, that where I am you may

be also. 4 And you know the way where I am going." 5 Thomas said to him, "Lord, we do not know where you are going; how can we know the way?" 6 Jesus said to him, "I am the way, and the truth, and the life; no one comes to the Father, but by me. 7 If you had known me, you would have known my Father also; henceforth you know him and have seen him."

8 Philip said to him, "Lord, show us the Father, and we shall be satisfied." 9 Jesus said to him, "Have I been with you so long, and yet you do not know me, Philip? He who has seen me has seen the Father; how can you say 'Show us the Father'? 10 Do you not believe that I am in the Father and the Father in me? The words that I say to you I do not speak on my own authority; but the Father who dwells in me does his works. 11 Believe me that I am in the Father and the Father in me; or else believe me for the sake of the works themselves.

12 Truly, truly, I say to you, he who believes in me will also do the works that I do; and greater works than these will he do, because I go to the Father. 13 Whatever you ask in my name, I will do it, that the Father may be glorified in the Son; 14 if you ask anything in my name, I will do it.

15 "If you love me, you will keep my commandments. 16 And I will pray the Father, and he will give you another Counsellor, to be with you for ever, 17 even the Spirit of truth, whom the world

cannot receive, because it neither sees him nor knows him; you know him, for he dwells with you, and will be in you.

18 "I will not leave you desolate; I will come to you. 19 Yet a little while, and the world will see me no more, but you will see me; because I live, you will live also. 20 In that day you will know that I am in my Father, and you in me, and I in you. 21 He who has my commandments and keeps them, he it is who loves me; and he who loves me will be loved by my Father, and I will love him and manifest myself to him." 22 Judas (not Iscariot) said to him, "Lord, how is it that you will manifest yourself to us, and not to the world?" 23 Jesus answered him, "If a man loves me, he will keep my word, and my Father will love him, and we will come to him and make our home with him. 24 He who does not love me does not keep my words; and the word which you hear is not mine but the Father's who sent me.

25 "These things I have spoken to you, while I am still with you. 26 But the Counsellor, the Holy Spirit, whom the Father will send in my name, he will teach you all things, and bring to your remembrance all that I have said to you. 27 Peace I leave with you; my peace I give to you; not as the world gives do I give to you. Let not your hearts be troubled, neither let them be afraid. 28 You have heard me say to you, "I go away, and I will come to you." If you loved me, you would have rejoiced, because I go to

the Father; for the Father is greater than I. 29 And now I have told you before it takes place, so that when it does take place, you may believe. 30 I will no longer talk much with you, for the ruler of this world is coming. He has no power over me; 31 but I do as the Father has commanded me, so that the world may know that I love the Father. Rise, let us go hence.

15. "I am the true vine, and my Father is the vine dresser. 2 Every branch of mine that bears no fruit, he takes away, and every branch that does bear fruit he prunes, that it may bear more fruit. 3 You are already made clean by the word which I have spoken to you. 4 Abide in me, and I in you. As the branch cannot bear fruit by itself, unless it abides in the vine, neither can you, unless you abide in me. 5 I am the vine, you are the branches. He who abides in me, and I in him, he it is that bears much fruit, for apart from me you can do nothing. 6 If a man does not abide in me, he is cast forth as a branch and withers; and the branches are gathered, thrown into the fire and burned. 7 If you abide in me, and my words abide in you, ask whatever you will, and it shall be done for you. 8 By this my Father is glorified, that you bear much fruit, and so prove to be my disciples. 9 As the Father has loved me, so have I loved you; abide in my love. 10 If you keep my commandments, you will abide in my love just as

I have kept my Father's commandments and abide in his love. 11 These things I have spoken to you, that my joy may be in you and that your joy may be full.

12 "This is my commandment, that you love one another as I have loved you. 13 Greater love has no man than this, that a man lay down his life for his friends. 14 You are my friends if you do what I command you. 15 No longer do I call you servants, for the servant does not know what his master is doing; but I have called you friends, for all that I have heard from my Father I have made known to you. 16 You did not choose me, but I chose you and appointed you that you should go and bear fruit and that your fruit should abide; so that whatever you ask the Father in my name, he may give it to you. 17 This I command you, to love one another.

18 "If the world hates you, know that it has hated me before it hated you. 19 If you were of the world, the world would love its own; but because you are not of the world, but I chose you out of the world, therefore the world hates you. 20 Remember the word that I said to you, 'A servant is not greater than his master.' If they persecuted me, they will persecute you; if they kept my word, they will keep yours also. 21 But all this they will do to you on my account, because they do not know him who sent me. 22 If I had not come and spoken to them, they would not have sin; but now they have no excuse for

their sin. 23 He who hates me hates my Father also. 24 If I had not done among them the works which no one else did, they would not have sin; but now they have seen and hated both me and my Father. 25 It is to fulfil the word that is written in their law, 'They hated me without a cause.' 26 But when the Counsellor comes whom I shall send to you from the Father, even the Spirit of truth, who proceeds from the Father, he will bear witness to me; 27 and you also are witnesses, because you have been with me from the beginning.

16. "I have said all this to you to keep you from falling away. 2 They will put you out of the synagogues; indeed, the hour is coming when whoever kills you will think he is offering service to God. 3 And they will do this because they have not known the Father, nor me. 4 But I have said these things to you, that when their hour comes you may remember that I told you of them.

"I did not say these things to you from the beginning, because I was with you. 5 But now I am going to him who sent me; yet none of you asks me, 'Where are you going?' 6 But because I have said these things to you, sorrow has filled your hearts. 7 Nevertheless I tell you the truth: it is to your advantage that I go away, for if I do not go away, the Counsellor will not come to you; but if I go, I will send him to you. 8 And when he comes, he will convince the world concerning sin and righteousness and judgement: 9 concerning sin, because they do not believe in me; 10 concerning righteousness, because I go to the Father, and you will see me no more; 11 concerning judgement, because the ruler of this world is judged.

12 "I have yet many things to say to you, but you cannot bear them now. 13 When the Spirit of truth comes, he will guide you into all the truth; for he will not speak on his own authority, but whatever he hears he will speak, and he will declare to you the things that are to come. 14 He will glorify me, for he will take what is mine and declare it to you. 15 All that the Father has is mine; therefore I said that he will take what is mine and declare it to you.

16 "A little while, and you will see me no more; again a little while, and you will see me." 17 Some of his disciples said to one another, "What is this that he says to us, 'A little while and you will not see me, and again a little while, and you will see me'; and, 'because I go to the Father'?" 18 They said, "What does he mean by 'a little while'? We do not know what he means." 19 Jesus knew that they wanted to ask him; so he said to them, "Is this what you are asking yourselves, what I meant by saying, 'A little while, and you will not see me, and again a little while, and you will see me'? 20 Truly, truly, I say to you, you will weep and lament, but the world will rejoice; you will be sorrowful, but your sorrow will

turn into joy. 21 When a woman is in travail she has sorrow, because her hour has come; but when she is delivered of the child, she no longer remembers the anguish, for joy that a child is born into the world. 22 So you have sorrow now, but I will see you again and your hearts will rejoice, and no one will take your joy from you. 23 In that day you will ask nothing of me. Truly, truly, I say to you, if you ask anything of the Father, he will give it to you in my name. 24 Hitherto you have asked nothing in my name; ask, and you will receive, that your joy may be full.

25 "I have said this to you in figures; the hour is coming when I shall no longer speak to you in figures but tell you plainly of the Father. 26 In that day you will ask in my name; and I do not say to you that I shall pray the Father for you; 27 for the Father himself loves you, because you have loved me and have believed that I came from the Father. 28 I came from the Father and have come into the world; again, I am leaving the world and going to the Father."

29 His disciples said, "Ah, now you are speaking plainly, not in any figure! 30 Now we know that you know all things, and need none to question you; by this we believe that you came from God." 31 Jesus answered them, "Do you now believe? 32 The hour is coming, indeed it has come, when you will be scattered, every man to his home, and will leave me alone; yet I am not alone, for the Father is with me.

33 I have said this to you, that in me you may have peace. In the world you have tribulation; but be of good cheer, I have overcome the world."

Matthew 26. 26 – 29   (RSV)
26 Now as they were eating, Jesus took bread, and blessed, and broke it and gave it to his disciples and said, "Take, eat; this is my body." 27 And he took a cup, and when he had given thanks he gave it to them, saying, "Drink of it, all of you; 28 for this is my blood of the covenant, which is poured out for many for the forgiveness of sins. 29 I tell you I shall not drink again of this fruit of the vine until that day when I drink it new with you in my Father's kingdom."

Mount of Olives. Jesus' arrest

Matthew 26. 30 – 75   (RSV)
30 And when they had sung a hymn, they went out to the Mount of Olives. 31 Then Jesus said to them, "You will all fall away because of me this night; for it is written, 'I will strike the shepherd, and the sheep of the flock will be scattered.' 32 But after I am raised up, I will go before you to Galilee." 33 Peter declared to him, "Though they all fall away because of you, I will never fall away." 34 Jesus said to him, "Truly, I say to you, this very night, before the cock

crows, you will deny me three times." 35 Peter said to him, "Even if I must die with you, I will not deny you." . And so said all the disciples."

36 Then Jesus went with them to a place called Gethsemane, and he said to his disciples, "Sit here, while I go yonder and pray." 37 And taking with him Peter and the two sons of Zebedee, he began to be sorrowful and troubled. 38 Then he said to them, "My soul is very sorrowful, even to death; remain here, and watch with me." 39 And going a little farther he fell on his face and prayed, "My Father, if it be possible, let this cup pass from me; nevertheless, not as I will, but as thou wilt." 40 And he came to the disciples and found them sleeping; and he said to Peter, "So, could you not watch with me one hour? 41 Watch and pray that you may not enter into temptation; the spirit indeed is willing, but the flesh is weak." 42 Again, for the second time, he went away and prayed, "My Father, if this cannot pass unless I drink it, thy will be done." 43 And again he came and found them sleeping, for their eyes were heavy. 44 So, leaving them again, he went away and prayed for the third time, saying the same words. 45 Then he came to the disciples and said to them, "Are you still sleeping and taking your rest? Behold, the hour is at hand, and the Son of man is betrayed into the hands of sinners. 46 Rise, let us be going; see, my betrayer is at hand."

47 While he was still speaking, Judas came, one

of the twelve, and with him a great crowd with swords and clubs, from the chief priests and the elders of the people. 48 Now the betrayer had given them a sign, saying, "The one I shall kiss is the man; seize him." 49 And he came up to Jesus at once and said "Hail Master!" And he kissed him. 50 Jesus said to him, "Friend why are you here?" Then they came up and laid hands on Jesus and seized him. 51 And behold, one of those who were with Jesus stretched out his hand and drew his sword, and struck the slave of the high priest, and cut off his ear. 52 Then Jesus said to him, "Put your sword back into its place; for all who take the sword will perish by the sword. 53 Do you think that I cannot appeal to my Father, and he will at once send me more than twelve legions of angels? 54 But how then should the scriptures be fulfilled, that it must be so?" 55 At that hour Jesus said to the crowds, "Have you come out as against a robber, with swords and clubs to capture me? Day after day I sat in the temple teaching, and you did not seize me. 56 But all this has taken place, that the scriptures of the prophets might be fulfilled." Then all the disciples forsook him and fled.

57 Then those who had seized Jesus led him to Caiaphas the high priest, where the scribes and the elders had gathered. 58 But Peter followed him at a distance, as far as the courtyard of the high priest, and going inside he sat with the guards to see the

end. 59 Now the chief priests and the whole council sought false testimony against Jesus that they might put him to death, 60 but they found none, though many false witnesses came forward. At last two came forward 61 and said, "This fellow said, 'I am able to destroy the temple of God, and to build it in three days.'" 62 And the high priest stood up and said, "Have you no answer to make? What is it that these men testify against you?" 63 But Jesus was silent. And the high priest said to him, "I adjure you by the living God, tell us if you are the Christ, the Son of God." 64 Jesus said to him, "You have said so. But I tell you, hereafter you will see the Son of man seated at the right hand of Power, and coming on the clouds of heaven."

65 Then the high priest tore his robes, and said, "He has uttered blasphemy. Why do we still need witnesses? You have now heard his blasphemy. 66 What is your judgement?" They answered, "He deserves death." 67 Then they spat in his face, and struck him; and some slapped him, 68 saying, "Prophesy to us, you Christ! Who is it that struck you?"

69 Now Peter was sitting outside in the courtyard. And a maid came up to him, and said, "You also were with Jesus the Galilean." 70 But he denied it before them all, saying "I do not know what you mean." 71 And when he went out to the porch, another maid saw him, and she said to the

bystanders, "This man was with Jesus of Nazareth." 72 And again he denied it with an oath, "I do not know the man." 73 After a little while the bystanders came up and said to Peter, "Certainly you are also one of them, for your accent betrays you." 74 Then he began to invoke a curse on himself and to swear, "I do not know the man." And immediately the cock crowed. 75 And Peter remembered the saying of Jesus, "Before the cock crows, you will deny me three times." And he went out and wept bitterly.

Examination by Pilate. Judas

Matthew 27. 1 – 21   (RSV)
When morning came, all the chief priests and the elders of the people took counsel against Jesus to put him to death: 2 and they bound him and led him away and delivered him to Pilate the governor.

3 When Judas, his betrayer, saw that he was condemned, he repented and brought back the thirty pieces of silver to the chief priests and the elders, 4 saying, "I have sinned in betraying innocent blood." They said, "What is that to us? See to it yourself." 5 And throwing down the pieces of silver in the temple, he departed; and he went and hanged himself. 6 But the chief priests, taking the pieces of silver, said, "It is not lawful to put them into the treasury, since

they are blood money."

7 So they took counsel, and bought with them the potters field, to bury strangers in. 8 Therefore that field has been called the Field of Blood to this day. 9 Then was fulfilled what had been spoken by the prophet Jeremiah, saying, "And they took the thirty pieces of silver, the price of him on whom a price had been set by some of the sons of Israel, 10 and they gave them for the potters field, as the Lord directed me."

11 Now Jesus stood before the governor; and the governor asked him, "Are you the King of the Jews?" Jesus said, "You have said so." 12 But when he was accused by the chief priests and elders, he made no answer. 13 Then Pilate said to him, "Do you not hear how many things they testify against you?" 14 But he gave him no answer, not even to a single charge; so that the governor wondered greatly.

15 Now at the feast the governor was accustomed to release for the crowd any one prisoner whom they wanted. 16 And they had then a notorious prisoner, called Barabbas. 17 So when they had gathered, Pilate said to them, "Whom do you want me to release for you, Barabbas or Jesus who is called Christ?" 18 For he knew that it was out of envy that they had delivered him up. 19 Besides, while he was sitting on the judgement seat, his wife sent word to him, "Have nothing to do with

that righteous man, for I have suffered much over him today in a dream." 20 Now the chief priests and the elders persuaded the people to ask for Barabbas and destroy Jesus. 21 The governor again said to them, "Which of the two do you want me to release for you?" And they said, "Barabbas".

John 19. 1 – 16 (RSV)

Then Pilate took Jesus and scourged him. 2 And the soldiers plaited a crown of thorns, and put it on his head, and arrayed him in a purple robe; 3 they came up to him saying "Hail, King of the Jews!" and struck him with their hands. 4 Pilate went out again and said to them, "See, I am bringing him out to you, that you may know that I find no crime in him." 5 So Jesus came out, wearing the crown of thorns and the purple robe. Pilate said to them, "Behold, the man!" 6 When the chief priests and the officers saw him, they cried out, "Crucify him, crucify him!" Pilate said to them, "Take him yourselves and crucify him, for I find no crime in him." 7 The Jews answered him, "We have a law, and by that law he ought to die, because he has made himself the Son of God." 8 When Pilate heard these words, he was the more afraid; 9 he entered the praetorium again and said to Jesus, "Where are you from?" But Jesus gave no answer. 10 Pilate therefore said to him, "You will not speak to me? Do you not know that I have power to release you, and power to crucify you?" 11 Jesus answered him, "You would have no power over me unless it had been given you from above; therefore he who delivered me to you has the greater sin."

12 Upon this Pilate sought to release him, but the Jews cried out, "If you release this man, you are not Caesar's friend; every one who makes himself the King sets himself against Caesar." 13 When Pilate heard these words, he brought Jesus out and sat down on the judgement seat at a place called The Pavement, and in Hebrew, Gabbatha. 14 Now it was the day of Preparation of the Passover; it was about the sixth hour. He said to the Jews, "Behold your King!" 15 They cried out, "Away with him, away with him, crucify him!" Pilate said to them, "Shall I crucify your King?" The chief priests answered, "We have no king but Caesar." 16 Then he handed him over to them to be crucified.

Crucifixion

Matthew 27. 32 – 43   (RSV)
32 As they went out, they came upon a man of Cyrene, Simon by name; this man they compelled to carry his cross. 33 And when they came to a place called Golgotha (which means the place of a skull), 34 they offered him wine to drink, mingled with gall; but when he tasted it, he would not drink it. 34 And when they had crucified him, they divided his

garments among them by casting lots; 35 then they sat down and kept watch over him there. 36 And over his head they put the charge against him, which read, "This is Jesus the King of the Jews." 38 Then two robbers were crucified with him, one on the right and one on the left. 39 And those who passed by derided him, wagging their heads 40 and saying, "You who would destroy the temple and build it in three days, save yourself. If you are the Son of God, come down from the cross." 41 So also the chief priests, with the scribes and elders, mocked him, saying, 42 "He saved others; he cannot save himself. He is the King of Israel; let him come down now from the cross, and we will believe in him. 43 He trusts in God; let God deliver him now if he desires him; for he said, 'I am the Son of God.'"

Luke 23. 39 – 43 (RSV)

39 One of the criminals who were hanged railed at him, saying, "Are you not the Christ? Save yourself and us!" 40 But the other rebuked him, saying, "Do you not fear God, since you are under the same sentence of condemnation? 41 And we indeed justly; for we are receiving the due reward of our deeds; but this man has done nothing wrong." 42 And he said, "Jesus, remember me when you come into your kingdom." 43 And he said to him, "Truly I say to you, today you will be with me in Paradise."

John 19. 25 – 27 (RSV)

25   So the soldiers did this. But standing by the cross of Jesus were his mother, and his mother's sister, Mary the wife of Clopas, and Mary Magdalene.   26   when Jesus saw his mother, and the disciple whom he loved standing near, he said to his mother, "Woman, behold your son!"   27   Then he said to the disciple, "Behold your mother!" And from that hour the disciple took her to his own home.

Mark 15. 33 – 39 (RSV)

33   And when the sixth hour had come, there was darkness over the whole land until the ninth hour.   34   And at the ninth hour Jesus cried with a loud voice, "Eloi, Eloi, lama sabachtani?" Which means, "My God, my God, why hast thou forsaken me?"   35 And some of the bystanders hearing it said, "Behold, he is calling Elijah."   36   And one ran and, filling a sponge full of vinegar, put it on a reed and gave it to him to drink, saying, "Wait, let us see whether Elijah will come to take him down."   37   And Jesus uttered a loud cry, and breathed his last.   38   and the curtain of the temple was torn in two, from top to bottom.   39 And when the centurion, who stood facing him, saw that he thus breathed his last, he said, "Truly this man was the Son of God!"

The tomb

Luke 23. 50 – 56 (RSV)

50 Now there was a man named Joseph from the Jewish town of Arimathea. He was a member of the council, a good and righteous man, 51 who had not consented to their purpose and deed, and he was looking for the kingdom of God. 52 This man went to Pilate and asked for the body of Jesus. 53 Then he took it down and wrapped it in a linen shroud, and laid him in a rock-hewn tomb, where no one had ever yet been laid. 54 It was the day of Preparation, and the sabbath was beginning. 55 The women who had come with him from Galilee followed, and saw the tomb, and how his body was laid; 56 then they returned and prepared spices and ointments.

On the sabbath they rested according to the commandment.

Matthew 27. 62 – 66   (RSV)

62 Next day, that is, after the day of Preparation, the chief priests and the Pharisees gathered before Pilate 63 and said, "Sir, we remember how that impostor said, while he was still alive, 'After three days I will rise again.' 64 Therefore order the sepulchre to be made secure until the third day, lest his disciples go and steal him away, and tell the people, 'He has risen from the dead, and the last fraud will be worse than the first." 65 Pilate said to

them, "You have a guard of soldiers; go, make it as secure as you can." 66 So they went and made the sepulchre secure by sealing the stone and setting a guard.

The appearances

John 20. 1 – 18   (RSV)

Now on the first day of the week Mary Magdalene came to the tomb early, while it was still dark, and saw that the stone had been taken away from the tomb. 2 So she ran, and went to Simon Peter and the other disciple, the one whom Jesus loved, and said to them, "They have taken the Lord out of the tomb, and we do not know where they have laid him." 3 Peter then came out with the other disciple, and they went toward the tomb. 4 They both ran, but the other disciple outran Peter and reached the tomb first; 5 and stooping to look in, he saw the linen cloths lying there, but he did not go in. 6 Then Simon Peter came, following him, and went into the tomb; he saw the linen cloths lying, 7 and the napkin, which had been on his head, not lying with the linen cloths but rolled up in a place by itself. 8 Then the other disciple, who reached the tomb first, also went in, and he saw and believed; 9 for as yet they did not know the scripture, that he must rise from the dead. 10 Then the disciples went back to their homes.

11   But Mary stood weeping outside the tomb, and as she wept she stooped to look into the tomb; 12   And she saw two angels in white sitting where the body of Jesus had lain, one at the head and one at the feet. 13   They said to her, "Woman, why are you weeping?" She said to them, "Because they have taken my Lord, and I do not know where they have laid him." 14 Saying this, she turned round and saw Jesus standing, but she did not know that it was Jesus. 15   Jesus said to her, "Woman, why are you weeping? Whom do you seek?" Supposing him to be the gardener, she said to him, "Sir, if you have carried him away, tell me where you have laid him, and I will take him away."   16   Jesus said to her, "Mary." She turned and said to him in Hebrew, "Rabboni!" (which means Teacher).   17   Jesus said to her, "Do not hold me, for I have not yet ascended to the Father; but go to my brethren and say to them, I am ascending to my Father and your Father, to my God and your God." 18   Mary Magdalene went and said to the disciples, "I have seen the Lord"; and she told them that he had said these things to her.

Luke 24. 13 – 35 (RSV)

13 That very day two of them were going to a village named Emmaus, about seven miles from Jerusalem, 14 and talking with each other about all these things that had happened. 15 While they were talking and discussing together, Jesus himself drew near and

went with them. 16 But their eyes were kept from recognising him. 17 And he said to them, "What is this conversation which you are holding with each other as you walk?" And they stood still, looking sad. 18 Then one of them, named Clopas, answered him, "Are you the only visitor to Jerusalem who does not know the things that have happened there in these days?" 19 And he said to them, "What things?" And they said to him, "Concerning Jesus of Nazareth, who was a prophet mighty in deed and word before God and all the people, 20 and how our chief priests and rulers delivered him up to be condemned to death, and crucified him. 21 But we had hoped that he was the one to redeem Israel. Yes, and besides all this, it is now the third day since this happened. 22 Moreover, some women of our company amazed us. They were at the tomb early in the morning 23 and did not find his body; and they came back saying that they had even seen a vision of angels, who said that he was alive. 24 Some of those who were with us went to the tomb, and found it just as the women had said; but him they did not see." 25 And he said to them, "O foolish men, and slow of heart to believe all that the prophets have spoken! 26 Was it not necessary that the Christ should suffer these things and enter into his glory?" 27 And beginning with Moses and all the prophets, he interpreted to them in all the scriptures the things concerning himself.

28 So they drew near to the village to which they were going. He appeared to be going further, 29 but they constrained him, saying, "Stay with us, for it is toward evening and the day is now far spent." So he went in to stay with them. 30 When he was at table with them, he took the bread and blessed, and broke it, and gave it to them. 31 And their eyes were opened and they recognised him; and he vanished out of their sight. 32 They said to each other, "Did not our hearts burn within us while he talked to us on the road, while he opened to us the scriptures?" 33 And they rose that same hour and returned to Jerusalem; and they found the eleven gathered together and those who were with them, 34 who said "The Lord has risen indeed, and has appeared to Simon!" 35 Then they told what had happened on the road, and how he was known to them in the breaking of the bread.

John 20. 19 – 29 (RSV)

19 On the evening of that day, the first day of the week, the doors being shut where the disciples were, for fear of the Jews, Jesus came and stood among them and said to them, "Peace be with you." 20 When he had said this, he showed them his hands and his side. Then the disciples were glad when they saw the Lord. 21 Jesus said to them again,"Peace be with you. As the Father has sent me, even so I send you." 22 And when he had said this, he

breathed on them, and said to them, "Receive the Holy Spirit. 23 If you forgive the sins of any, they are forgiven; if you retain the sins of any, they are retained."

24 Now Thomas, one of the twelve, called the Twin, was not with them when Jesus came. 25 So the other disciples told him, "We have seen the Lord." But he said to them, "Unless I see in his hands the print of the nails, and place my finger in the mark of the nails, and place my hand in his side, I will not believe."

26 Eight days later, his disciples were again in the house, and Thomas was with them. The doors were shut, but Jesus came and stood among them, and said, "Peace be with you." 27 Then he said to Thomas, "Put your finger here, and see my hands; and put out your hand, and place it in my side; do not be faithless, but believing." 28 Thomas answered him, "My Lord and my God!" 29 Jesus said to him, "Have you believed because you have seen me? Blessed are those who have not seen and yet believe."

Chapter XVIII
About the Passion

There is no story I know that matches that of the Passion in intensity. Every emotion is drunk and drained to the last drop. In the garden of Gethsemane Jesus allows himself, in the fear that must have beset him, the indulgence of asking God if there is any way His purpose could be fulfilled other than through the terrifying ordeal that awaits him. "Nevertheless, not as I will, but as thou wilt."

But, as Jesus must have already known in his heart, anything less would have fallen short of that ultimate demonstration that God's love and its expression are more important than anything, including any experience, however terrible. Once having irrevocably committed himself to the final pursuit of that course, Jesus just wishes it to take place without delay. "What you are going to do, do quickly" he says to Judas.

Beyond the all-important public declaration to the Temple rulers of the divinity of his nature and his message, he makes no response to any of the accusations and charges against him, just waiting for the destined events to unfold.

The most vivid detail fills the narrative, detail that proclaims itself as from real events, from the heartrending 'And Peter "went out and wept bitterly"', to Pilate's wife sending to her husband to have nothing to do with the charges brought against Jesus. One wonders how that story came to be known – perhaps through a slave of Pilate's wife who later became a Christian?

In respect of Judas, some years ago I saw Stephen Adly Guirgis's stunning, hilarious, and intensely moving play *The Last Days of Judas Iscariot*. In the likeness and vernacular of the downtown New York subway, the play is set in Purgatory, the staging point for Heaven or Hell, a place largely occupied, it seems, by individuals who have not yet made up their minds which way they are going, up or down. A trial is in process, a review of the case of Judas Iscariot, currently Satan's prize trophy, a review summoned on a writ signed by God himself.

Throughout most of the action Judas himself kneels frozen before the audience, hands spread, wide eyes staring, in the catatonic trance induced by realisation of what he has done.

One by one the witnesses are called – Judas' mother, Caiaphas the Elder, Pilate, Sigmund Freud, Satan himself. Gradually it emerges that the sin barring Judas' entry to Heaven is despair. "Your client," Satan responds with devastatingly casual confidence to the impassioned plea of Judas' Counsel for his release, "is free to leave whenever he wants".

Jesus, permanently holding a bucket, approaches Judas' kneeling figure. He calls to him repeatedly, and gradually Judas emerges from his trance only to recoil furiously at the sight of Jesus.

"DON'T ----------------- TOUCH ME." Get away! Don't come near!

Again and again Jesus pleads with him to leave the state he is in and rejoin him, to, each time, be passionately repulsed. When Judas most needed him Jesus abandoned him, Judas accuses. He helped everybody else but he has allowed Judas to make the dreadful mistakes he has. Why didn't he tell him and stop him, instead of abandoning him, from coming to the terrible place he now is?

He has always been with him, Jesus responds. If he, Jesus, could have acted in any way that would have made Judas behave differently, does Judas imagine for a moment that he would not have done so?

"What," says Jesus, "if I were to tell you that you are not here? That you are with me in my Kingdom even now, and that you have been there since the morning of my Ascension and that you have never left?"

Judas spits in his face.

He has betrayed the thing he loves and now he cannot bear to look at it.

Jesus does not wipe his face.

Satan appears.

"Do you know him?" asks Jesus. "Call unto him. Touch him. He is not there. Because he does not exist, Judas."

Gradually Judas starts to revert to his catatonic state, his responses becoming more and more distant. Wearily Jesus takes off his shirt, dips it into the bucket, and starts to wash Judas' feet.

In relation to the Resurrection, my position on miracles remains as always; but I have never understood the importance attached to the physical in respect of it. We all accept the reality of the spirit, do we not? We believe the continued existence of those we love who have died? Christ is alive for us, though not here? Why do we need something more? Life after death is surely in a different dimension to that we have now?

In respect of the resurrection of Christ's body, as I say, my position on miracles remains but, to me, the simple disappearance of his body is, in itself, already a miracle. The one thing the Jewish religious authorities were determined should not take place, with guards posted to ensure it did not, that is just what happened, with the consequences exactly as they had foreseen.

Piero de la Francesca's painting wonderfully captures the miracle. Ranks of guards, and as they succumb to the inevitable sleep, Jesus simply steps up out of the tomb behind them, unstoppable.

Bernard Shaw has one of the characters in his 'St Joan' describe miracles as 'any event that creates faith.' He probably meant it mischievously, but is there any event about which that is more true than this one? Even with their acceptance of the reality of spiritual existence, people might have struggled to believe that Christ had triumphed, with the mockery of the scribes and Pharisees, and after the terrible death they had witnessed, but with his body gone... You can still feel the thrill of that discovery.

When it came to Christ's appearances to his disciples after his death, in most of them there is a sensitivity about his physical body. "Don't touch me" says Jesus to Mary when she suddenly recognises him in the person she had taken for the gardener. Thomas (can't we all identify with him) dismisses the other disciples' accounts of Jesus' appearance to them with the words "Unless I see in his hands the print of the nails, and put my finger into the print of the nails, and put my hand into his side, I will not believe."

When Jesus appears to them again, this time with Thomas present, and says to him "Reach here your finger and behold my hands, and reach here your finger and put it into my side: and be not faithless but believing", Thomas responds "My Lord and my God". Harold Stringer points out that there is no reference to his then touching Jesus. Does this not describe Thomas acknowledging the reality of Christ's living spirit without the need to physically touch him?

Jesus then says "Thomas, because you have seen me, you have believed. Blessed are they that have not seen me and yet have believed." I know there is an account in John about Jesus appearing to disciples on the beach, and eating breakfast with them, with them initially too much in awe to address him.

The Road to Emmaus is, for me, another favourite story, again grippingly captured in Caravaggio's painting in the National Gallery. The elbow of one of the disciples looks to be about to split the canvas, drawn back so violently towards us in the shock of the sudden recognition at the breaking of the bread. The other spreads his arms cross-like in amazement.

When a school party was asked what they thought the picture was about the response was "well, *she*," (referring to Jesus) "is obviously having a row with the other ones." Jesus is indeed very unlike any traditional representation, a round, chubby, beardless face, with flowing, rather feminine, hair, wonderfully evoking the disciples initially failing to recognise him.

That failure to see something absolutely in your face, until afterwards, when it is so obvious, is an experience I have had a good number of times, when it is perhaps too late – the something is too big to engage with immediately? One's attention is still too focussed on one's own little plans?

The innkeeper, I think, stands for all of us, staring bemusedly at the Christ figure, dimly aware that there is something of significance here (but what?) the light from the side throwing by chance a silhouette of his cap in a halo shaped shadow on the wall behind Christ's head.

Matthew 28. 16 -20 (RSV)
16 Now the eleven disciples went to Galilee, to the mountain to which Jesus had directed them. 17 And when they saw him they worshipped him; but some doubted. 18 And Jesus came and said to them, "All authority in heaven and on earth has been given to me. 19 Go therefore and make disciples of all nations, baptising them in the name of the Father and of the Son and of the Holy Spirit, 20 teaching them to observe all that I have commanded you; and lo, I am with you always, to the close of the age."

Afterward

Chapter XIX
The beginning

My predominant feeling when reading Acts is gratitude; to the men and women who chose not just to live the faith they had gained from Christ's life and message, but to proclaim it.

It would have been so easy for the faithful to have incorporated that faith into their private lives and to have discreetly lived it below the radar, largely in the privacy of their own homes. If that had happened the Christian message would, from the point of view of the authorities, have appeared to have sunk without trace. Killing Jesus had apparently successfully also killed his message.

There would have been no need of a Saul of Tarsus, breathing fire, to hound his intolerable followers. No conversion? No early church established as we know it? With what implications for Christianity being chosen as the unifying force for the Roman empire? And with what consequent implications for our own encounter with it? But it appears that it was not even a temptation for those followers to look for a quiet life and keep their faith to themselves. An overwhelming compulsion drove them to want to proclaim it wherever and whenever the opportunity arose.

Almost from day one it was trouble – vilification, threats, exclusion, beatings and beatings up, arrest, imprisonment, death.

The events of Pentecost, the speaking in tongues, Peter's inspirational speech to the astonished observers, cut to the quick by the guilt they felt at their part, either actively or in absentia, in Jesus' death, leading to some 3,000 people coming forward for baptism and commitment to the new faith – this appears to have largely escaped the notice of the Temple authorities.

Impelled by the dynamic momentum of conversion commitment, there followed the inspirational and poignant attempt by large numbers of people to give themselves over totally to living their life in fulfilment of their faith with abandonment of personal possessions, worshipping and sharing bread together with everything dedicated to the common good, an initiative, as described earlier, that inevitably ran into such completely understandable human problems and frailties, but was no less a precious response of love to Christ's call.

Again, it appears this does not seem to have particularly come to the attention of or been of interest to the authorities.

Soon, however, a familiar pattern was starting to

re-emerge; Peter and John teaching in the Temple. I imagine the Temple space to have been a bit like Hyde Park Corner, a forum open to speakers of all kinds. So, again, a particular pair of speakers would not necessarily attract the attention of the authorities.

Then came the lame man healed by Peter and John, and the consequent crowds rushing together. Now the authorities woke up. They arrested Peter and John for teaching of Jesus and the resurrection from the dead. Next morning they faced the full establishment of the Temple – Annas the High Priest, Caiaphas, and "all who were of the high priestly family".

"By what power or by what name did you do this?" they are asked. Peter's response is characteristically uncompromising.

Acts 4. 8 – 12   (RSV)
8   Then Peter, filled with the Holy Spirit, said to them, "Rulers of the people and elders, 9 if we are being examined today concerning a good deed done to a cripple, by what means this man has been healed, 10 be it known to you all, and to all the people of Israel, that by the name of Jesus Christ of Nazareth, whom you crucified, whom God raised from the dead, by him this man is standing before you well. 11 This is the stone which was rejected by you builders, but which has become the head of the

corner. 12 And there is salvation in no one else, for there is no other name under heaven given among men by which we must be saved."

The next statement is, I think, very significant.

Acts 4. 13   (RSV)
13 Now when they saw the boldness of Peter and John, and perceived that they were uneducated, common men, they wondered; and they recognised that they had been with Jesus.

It must have indeed been deeply unsettling to hear such apparently ordinary, unsophisticated country folk expressing themselves with such telling clarity and such rock-like conviction.

The old problem was back. They had to put a stop to it, this threat to their authority, this ministry of Jesus, but how were they to justify it, with the healed man, witnessed by the crowds, standing in front of them? They fell back on threats, although probably, from past experience, they, correctly, did not have much hope of this solving the problem.

Acts 4. 18 – 31 (RSV)
18 So they called them and charged them not to speak or teach at all in the name of Jesus. 19 But Peter and John answered them, "Whether it is right in the sight of God to listen to you rather than to

God, you must judge; 20 for we cannot but speak of what we have seen and heard." 21 And when they had further threatened them, they let them go, finding no way to punish them because of the people; for all men praised God for what had happened. 22 For the man on whom this sign of healing was performed was more than forty years old.

23 When they were released they went to their friends and reported what the chief priests and the elders had said to them. 24 And when they heard it, they lifted their voices together to God and said, "Sovereign Lord, who didst make the heaven and the earth and the sea and everything in them, 25 who by the mouth of our father David, thy servant didst say by the Holy Spirit,

'Why did the Gentiles rage,

and the peoples imagine vain things?

26 The kings of the earth set themselves in array,

and the rulers were gathered together, against the Lord and against his Anointed –

27 for truly in this city there were gathered together against thy holy servant Jesus, whom thou didst anoint, both Herod and Pontius Pilate, with the Gentiles and the peoples of Israel, 28 to do whatever thy hand and thy plan had predestined to take place. 29 And now, Lord, look upon their threats, and grant to thy servants to speak thy word

with all boldness, 30 while thou stretchest out thy hand to heal, and signs and wonders are performed through the name of thy holy servant Jesus." 31 And when they had prayed, the place in which they were gathered together was shaken; and they were all filled with the Holy Spirit and spoke the word of God with boldness.

The momentum of proclaiming Christ's message rapidly increased. The apostles, it says, were all together in Solomon's portico. 'None of the rest dared to join them'. I wonder where I would have been.

Acts 5. 12 – 42 (RSV)

12   Now many signs and wonders were done among the people by the hands of the Apostles. And they were all together in Solomon's portico.   13 None of the rest dared join them, but the people held them in a high honour.   14   And more than ever believers were added to the Lord, multitudes both of men and women, 15 so that they even carried out the sick into the streets, and laid them on beds and pallets, that as Peter came by at least his shadow might fall on some of them. 16   The people also gathered from the towns around Jerusalem, bringing the sick and those afflicted with unclean spirits, and they were all healed.

17 But the high priest rose up and all who were

with him, that is the party of the Sadducees, and filled with jealousy 18 they arrested the apostles and put them in the common prison. 19 But at night an angel of the Lord opened the prison doors and brought them out and said, 20 "Go and stand in the temple and speak to the people all the words of this Life." 21 And when they heard this, they entered the temple at daybreak and taught.

Now the high priest came and those who were with him and called together the council and all the senate of Israel, and sent to the prison to have them brought. 22 But when the officers came, they did not find them in the prison, and they returned and reported, 23 "We found the prison securely locked and the sentries standing at the doors, but when we opened it we found no one inside." 24 Now when the captain of the temple and the chief priests heard these words, they were much perplexed about them, wondering what this would come to. 25 And some one came and told them, "The men whom you put in prison are standing in the temple and teaching the people." 26 Then the captain with the officers went and brought them, but without violence, for they were afraid of being stoned by the people.

27 And when they had brought them, they set them before the council. And the high priest questioned them, 28 saying, "We strictly charged you not to teach in this name, yet here you have filled Jerusalem with your teaching and you intend to

bring this man's blood upon us." 29 But Peter and the apostles answered, "We must obey God rather than men. 30 The God of our fathers raised Jesus whom you killed by hanging him on a tree. 31 God exalted him in his right hand as Leader and Saviour, to give repentance to Israel and forgiveness of sins. 32 And we are witnesses to these things, and so is the Holy Spirit whom God has given to those who obey him."

33 When they heard this they were enraged and wanted to kill them. 34 But a Pharisee in the council named Gamaliel, a teacher of the law, held in honour by all the people, stood up and ordered the men to be put outside for a while. 35 And he said to them, "Men of Israel, take care what you do with these men. 36 For before these days Theudas arose, giving himself out to be somebody, and a number of men, about four hundred, joined him; but he was slain and all who followed him were dispersed and came to nothing. 37 After him Judas the Galilean arose in the days of the census and drew away some of the people after him; he also perished, and all who followed him were scattered. 38 So in the present case I tell you, keep away from these men and let them alone; for if this plan for this undertaking is of men, it will fail; 39 But if it is of God, you will not be able to overthrow them. You might even be found opposing God!" 40 So they took his advice, and when they had called in the

apostles they beat them and charged them not to speak in the name of Jesus, and let them go. 41 Then they left the presence of the council, rejoicing that they were counted worthy to suffer dishonour for the name. 42 And every day in the temple and at home they did not cease teaching and preaching Jesus as the Christ.

"They beat them and let them go" – an instructive example of 'keeping away from them and letting them alone', the least you could expect for any making public of your faith in Christ.

Chapter XX
Faith and everyday life. Stephen. Paul

There follows, in the next verses of Acts, reference to a strange little issue. The new 'Christians' or 'Nazarene sect' were translating the meaning of their faith into everyday life. Penniless, helpless widows were no longer to be left to survive by begging for charity. They were to become part of the community's new responsibilities.

However, the issue that would have a long way to run was already making itself felt. All subscribers to the new faith were equal, but the Jewish ones to whom the message had originally been directed were surely, by definition, more equal, or at least more first in line, than Hellenist or Greek ones?

In fulfilment of Christ's bidding to be the servant of all, the apostles were serving at tables, but in the process were accused of not showing enough impartiality in respect of newcomers alongside ladies they had probably known since childhood. To address this problem, seven men were appointed to relieve the apostles of these duties, one of whom was Stephen, soon to become the first Christian martyr to follow in Christ's footsteps.

Acts 6. 1 – 15   (RSV)

Now in these days when the disciples were increasing in number, the Hellenists murmured against the Hebrews because their widows were neglected in the daily distribution. 2 And the twelve summoned the body of the disciples and said, "It is not right that we should give up preaching the word of God to serve tables. 3 Therefore, brethren, pick out from among you seven men of good repute, full of the Spirit and of wisdom, whom we may appoint to this duty. 4 But we will devote ourselves to prayer and to the ministry of the word." 5 And what they said pleased the whole multitude, and they chose Stephen, a man full of faith and of the Holy Spirit, and Philip, and Prochorus, and Nicanor, and Timon, and Parmenas, and Nicolaus, a proselyte of Antioch. 6 These they set before the apostles, and they prayed and laid their hands upon them.

7 And the word of God increased; and the number of the disciples multiplied greatly in Jerusalem, and a great many of the priests were obedient to the faith.

8 And Stephen, full of grace and power did great wonders and signs among the people. 9 Then some of those who belonged to the synagogue of the Freedmen (as it was called), and of the Cyrenians, and of the Alexandrians, and of those

from Cilicia and Asia, arose and disputed with Stephen. 10 But they could not withstand the wisdom and the Spirit with which he spoke. 11 Then they secretly instigated men who said, "We have heard him speak blasphemous words against Moses and God." 12 And they stirred up the people and the elders and the scribes, and they came upon him and seized him and brought him before the council, 13 and set up false witnesses who said, "This man never ceases to speak words against this holy place and the law; 14 for we have heard him say that this Jesus of Nazareth will destroy this place, and will change the customs which Moses delivered to us." 15 And gazing at him, all who sat in the council saw that his face was like the face of an angel.

"Is this so?" The high priest asks Stephen.

Stephen gives a long and learned reply showing how well he knows and understands the origins and background of his peoples, their beliefs and laws, identifying parallels that he will draw in respect of Jesus and where the people have ignored and set aside their major prophets such as, indeed, Moses. Then he turns to how the present Temple has repeated these errors.

Acts 7. 51 – 60 (RSV)
51 "You stiff-necked people, uncircumcised in heart

and ears, you always resist the Holy Spirit. As your fathers did, so do you. 52 Which of the prophets did not your fathers persecute? And they killed those who announced beforehand the coming of the Righteous One, whom you have now betrayed and murdered, 53 you who received the law as delivered by angels and did not keep it."

54 Now when they heard these things they were enraged, and they ground their teeth against him. 55 But he, full of the Holy Spirit, gazed into heaven and saw the glory of God, and Jesus standing at the right hand of God; 56 And he said, "Behold, I see the heavens opened, and the Son of man standing at the right hand of God." 57 But they cried out with a loud voice and stopped their ears and rushed together upon him. 58 Then they cast him out of the city and stoned him; and the witnesses laid down their garments at the feet of a young man named Saul. 59 And as they were stoning Stephen, he prayed, "Lord Jesus, receive my spirit." 60 And he knelt down and cried with a loud voice, "Lord do not hold this sin against them." And when he had said this, he fell asleep.

Enter Paul

Acts 8. 1 – 8   (RSV)
And Saul was consenting to his death.

And on that day a great persecution arose against the church in Jerusalem; and they were all scattered throughout the region of Judea and Samaria, except the apostles. 2 Devout men buried Stephen, and made great lamentation over him. 3 But Saul was ravaging the church, and entering house after house, he dragged off men and women and committed them to prison.

4 Now those who were scattered went about preaching the word. 5 Philip went down to a city of Samaria and proclaimed to them the Christ. 6 And the multitudes with one accord gave heed to what was said by Philip, when they heard him and saw the signs which he did. 7 For unclean spirits came out of many who were possessed, crying with a loud voice; and many who were paralysed or lame were healed. 8 So there was much joy in that city.

Acts 9. 1 – 19   (RSV)

But Saul, still breathing threats and murder against the disciples of the Lord went to the high priest 2 and asked him for letters to the synagogues at Damascus, so that if he found any belonging to the Way, men or women, he might bring them bound to Jerusalem. 3 Now as he journeyed he approached Damascus, and suddenly a light from heaven flashed about him, 4 And he fell to the ground and heard a voice saying to him, "Saul, Saul, why do you persecute me?" 5 And he said, " Who are you

Lord?" And he said, " I am Jesus, whom you are persecuting; 6 but arise and enter the city and you will be told what you are to do." 7 The men who were travelling with him stood speechless, hearing the voice but seeing no one. 8 Saul arose from the ground; and when his eyes were opened he could see nothing; so they led him by the hand and brought him into Damascus. 9 And for three days he was without sight, and neither ate nor drank.

10 Now there was a disciple at Damascus named Ananias. The Lord said to him in a vision, "Ananias". And he said, "Here I am, Lord." 11 And the Lord said to him, "Rise and go to the street called Straight, and inquire in the house of Judas for a man of Tarsus named Saul; for behold, he is praying, 12 and he has seen a man named Ananias come in and lay his hands on him so that he might regain his sight. 13 But Ananias answered, "Lord, I have heard from many about this man, how much evil he has done to thy saints at Jerusalem; 14 and here he has authority from the chief priests to bind all who call upon thy name." 15 But the Lord said to him, "Go, for he is a chosen instrument of mine to carry my name before the Gentiles and Kings and the sons of Israel; 16 for I will show him how much he must suffer for the sake of my name." 17 So Ananias departed and entered the house. And laying his hands on him he said, "Brother Saul, the Lord Jesus who appeared to you on the road by which

you came, has sent me that you may regain your sight and be filled with the Holy Spirit." 18 And immediately something like scales fell from his eyes and he regained his sight. Then he rose and was baptised, 19 and took food and was strengthened.

St Paul's spectacular conversion story is perhaps the least amazing thing about this astonishing man. So often the most passionate opponents of an idea are found vigorously trying to persecute out of others what they fear most in themselves.

My guess is that Paul, rock-like adherent, I suspect, of the most orthodox Jewish religious law and observances, had, when he first heard the intimation of Christ's message, with horror also heard the death knell of his own present convictions. The only answer was a complete shutdown of that consciousness and a crusade to eradicate the 'Nazarene sect' and its ideas. When he finally is brought to face himself on the Damascus road he must have been already poised for the 180 degree turn he then made.

It is irresistible not to imagine, a little, reception of the news in Temple circles. "He's doing WHAT?!"

St Paul's work starts, to the bewilderment and disbelief, too, of most Christians. So, too, starts Paul's life of adventure. Within weeks there is the first plot to kill him, and his dramatic escape.

Acts 9. 19 – 31 (RSV)

19 For several days he was with the disciples at Damascus. 20 And in the synagogues immediately he proclaimed Jesus, saying, "He is the Son of God." 21 And all who heard him were amazed and said, "Is not this the man who made havoc in Jerusalem of those who called on this name? And he has come here for this purpose to bring them bound before the chief priests." 22 But Saul increased all the more in strength, and confounded the Jews who lived in Damascus by proving that Jesus was the Christ.

23 When many days had passed, the Jews plotted to kill him, 24 but their plot became known to Saul. They were watching the gates day and night, to kill him; 25 but his disciples took him by night and let him down over the wall, lowering him in a basket.

26 And when he had come to Jerusalem he attempted to join the disciples; and they were all afraid of him for they did not believe that he was a disciple. 27 But Barnabas took him, and brought him to the apostles, and declared to them how on the road he had seen the Lord, who spoke to him, and how at Damascus he had preached boldly in the name of Jesus. 28 So he went in and out among them at Jerusalem, 29 preaching boldly in the name of the Lord. And he spoke and disputed against the Hellenists; but they were seeking to kill him. 30 And when the brethren knew it, they

brought him down to Caesarea, and sent him off to Tarsus.

31 So the church throughout all Judea and Galilee and Samaria had peace and was built up; and walking in the fear of the Lord and in the comfort of the Holy Spirit it was multiplied.

Acts makes no mention of it, but it appears from what Paul writes to the Galatians (1. 15 – 23) that after his conversion and his initial burst of preaching and evangelising, he took himself away to 'Arabia' (the desert?) – to take in fully what had happened to him and what it meant for his life? – to marinate in his new understanding?

He was away, at any rate, for some three years, when he made his way to Jerusalem and met Peter, although the other disciples were still extremely nervous of him. He seemingly then returned to Tarsus where Barnabas came looking for him to get his help for the work in Antioch. So Paul's preparation period was over and he travelled back to Antioch with Barnabas at the start of the partnership that was to bear so much fruit through so many trials, until its sad ending in disagreement a few years later.

Chapter XXI
Peter

Acts 10. 1 – 48 (RSV)

At Caesarea there was a man named Cornelius, a centurion of what was known as the Italian Cohort, 2 a devout man who feared God with all his household, gave alms liberally to the people, and prayed constantly to God. 3 About the ninth hour of the day he saw clearly in a vision an angel of God coming in and saying to him, "Cornelius". 4 And he stared at him in terror, and said, "What is it Lord?" And he said to him, "Your prayers and your alms have ascended as a memorial before God. 5 And now send men to Joppa, and bring one Simon who is called Peter; 6 he is lodging with Simon, a tanner, whose house is by the seaside" 7 When the angel who spoke to him had departed, he called two of his servants and a devout soldier from among those that waited on him, 8 and having related everything to them, he sent them to Joppa.

9 The next day, as they were on their journey and coming near the city, Peter went up on the house top to pray, about the sixth hour. 10 And he became hungry and desired something to eat; but while they were preparing it, he fell into a trance 11

and saw the heaven opened, and something descending, like a great sheet, let down by four corners upon the earth. 12 In it were all kinds of animals and reptiles and birds of the air. 13 And there came a voice to him, "Rise, Peter; kill and eat." 14 But Peter said, "No, Lord; for I have never eaten anything that is common or unclean." 15 And the voice came to him again a second time, "What God has cleansed, you must not call common." 16 This happened three times, and the thing was taken up at once to heaven.

17 Now while Peter was inwardly perplexed as to what the vision which he had seen might mean, behold, the men that were sent by Cornelius, having made inquiry for Simon's house, stood before the gate 18 and called out to ask whether Simon who was called Peter was lodging there. 19 And while Peter was pondering the vision the Spirit said to him, "Behold, three men are looking for you. 20 Rise and go down, and accompany them without hesitation; for I have sent them." 21 And Peter went down to the men and said, "I am the one you are looking for; what is the reason for your coming?" 22 And they said, "Cornelius, a centurion, an upright and God-fearing man, who is well spoken of by the whole Jewish nation, was directed by a holy angel to send for you to come to his house and to hear what you have to say." 23 So he called them in to be his guests.

The next day he rose and went off with them, and some of the brethren from Joppa accompanied him. 24 And on the following day they entered Caesarea. Cornelius was expecting them and had called together his kinsmen and close friends. 25 When Peter entered, Cornelius met him and fell down at his feet and worshipped him. 26 But Peter lifted him up, saying, "Stand up; I too am a man." 27 And as he talked with him he went in and found many persons gathered; 28 and he said to them, "You yourselves know how unlawful it is for a Jew to associate with or to visit any one of another nation; but God has shown me that I should not call any man common or unclean. 29 So when I was sent for, I came without objection. I ask then why you sent for me."

30 And Cornelius said, "Four days ago, about this hour, I was keeping the ninth hour of prayer in my house; and behold, a man stood before me in bright apparel, 31 saying, 'Cornelius, your prayer has been heard and your alms have been remembered before God. 32 Send therefore to Joppa and ask for Simon who is called Peter; he is lodging in the house of Simon, a tanner, by the seaside.' 33 So I sent to you at once, and you have been kind enough to come. Now therefore we are all here in the sight of God, to hear all that you have been commanded by the Lord."

34 And Peter opened his mouth and said: "Truly I

perceive that God shows no partiality, 35 but in every nation anyone who fears him and does what is right is acceptable to him. 36 You know the word which he sent to Israel, preaching good news of peace by Jesus Christ (he is Lord of all), 37 the word which was proclaimed throughout all Judea, beginning from Galilee after the baptism which John preached: 38 how God anointed Jesus of Nazareth with the Holy Spirit and with power; how he went about doing good and healing all that were oppressed by the devil, for God was with him. 39 And we are witnesses to all that he did both in the country of the Jews and in Jerusalem. They put him to death by hanging him on a tree; 40 but God raised him on the third day and made him manifest; 41 not to all the people but to us who were chosen by God as witnesses, who ate and drank with him after he rose from the dead 42 And he commanded us to preach to the people, and to testify that he is the one ordained by God to be judged of the living and the dead. 43 To him all the prophets bear witness that everyone who believes in him receives forgiveness of sins through his name."

44 While Peter was still saying this, the Holy Spirit fell on all who heard the word. 45 And the believers from among the circumcised who came with Peter were amazed, because the gift of the Holy Spirit had been poured out even on the Gentiles. 46 For they heard them speaking in tongues and

extolling God. Then Peter declared, 47 "Can anyone forbid water for baptising these people who have received the Holy Spirit just as we have?" 48 And he commanded them to be baptised in the name of Jesus Christ. Then they asked him to remain for some days.

I would have thought that blunt, outspoken (traditional?) Peter would have been amongst the most resistant and difficult to persuade that Jesus' message should not first of all go to the Jews, and, if at all, to the Gentiles only through their first submitting themselves to the Judaic law and observances. But it needs only one clear indication for him to adopt, wholesale, a radical new approach to the mission that now constitutes his life – the qualities of honesty, humility, courage, and big-heartedness that make him so lovable.

As might be expected, Peter's actions, reported in Jerusalem, cause a huge upheaval, and when he returns he finds himself in a storm of controversy and criticism.

So the turning point moment has arrived. Paul may be preaching to the Gentiles at the far edges of the world, but is the message now to go from here, Jerusalem, the centre and source of the new faith, not, as always understood, through the medium of Judaic law and observances, but, without reference to them, also directly to the polluting Gentile

251

masses? Again, I find it very moving that people who obviously had such intensely held views had also the humility to be prepared, unhesitatingly, to review them. Are we all so open hearted?

Acts 11. 1 – 18 (RSV)

Now the apostles and the brethren who were in Judea heard that the Gentiles also had received the word of God. 2 So when Peter went up to Jerusalem, the circumcision party criticised him, 3 saying, "Why did you go to uncircumcised men and eat with them?" 4 But Peter began and explained to them in order: 5 "I was in the city of Joppa praying; and in a trance I saw a vision, something descending, like a great sheet, let down from heaven by four corners; and it came down to me. 6 Looking at it closely I observed animals and beasts of prey and reptiles and birds of the air. 7 And I heard a voice saying to me, 'Rise, Peter; kill and eat.' 8 But I said, 'No Lord; for nothing common or unclean has ever entered my mouth.' 9 But the voice answered a second time from heaven, 'What God has cleansed you must not call common.' 10 This happened three times, and all was drawn up again into heaven. 11 At that very moment three men arrived at the house in which we were, sent to me from Caesarea. 12 And the Spirit told me to go with them, making no distinction. These six brethren also accompanied me, and we entered the man's house.

13   And he told us how he had seen the angel standing in his house and saying, 'Send to Joppa and bring Simon called Peter; 14 he will declare to you a message by which you will be saved, you and all your household.' 15   As I began to speak, the Holy Spirit fell on them just as on us at the beginning. 16 And I remembered the word of the Lord, how he said, 'John baptised with water, but you shall be baptised with the Holy Spirit.' 17 If then God gave the same gift to them as he gave to us when we believed in the Lord Jesus Christ, who was I that I could withstand God?" 18 When they heard this they were silenced. And they glorified God, saying, "Then to the Gentiles also God has granted repentance unto life."

The Word starts steadily to spread. I note mention of the first reference to the name 'Christians'

Acts 11. 19 – 30   (RSV)

19   Now those who were scattered because of the persecution that arose over Stephen travelled as far as Phoenicia and Cyprus and Antioch, speaking the word to none except Jews. 20 But there were some of them, men of Cyprus and Cyrene, who on coming to Antioch spoke to the Greeks also, preaching the Lord Jesus.   21 And the hand of the Lord was with them, and a great number that believed turned to the Lord.   22   News of this came to the ears of the

253

church in Jerusalem, and they sent Barnabas to Antioch. 23 When he came and saw the grace of God, he was glad; and he exhorted them all to remain faithful to the Lord with steadfast purpose; 24 for he was a good man, full of the Holy Spirit and of faith. And a large company was added to the Lord. 25 So Barnabas went to Tarsus to look for Saul; 26 and when he had found him, he brought him to Antioch. For a whole year they met with the church, and taught a large company of people; and in Antioch the disciples were for the first time called Christians.

27 Now in these days prophets came down from Jerusalem to Antioch. 28 And one of them named Agabus stood up and foretold by the Spirit that there would be a great famine over all the world; and this took place in the days of Claudius. 29 And the disciples determined, every one according to his ability, to send relief to the brethren who lived in Judea; 30 and they did so, sending it to the elders by the hand of Barnabas and Saul.

Chapter XXII
Harassment and
intimidation

The harassment and intimidation continues, borne with unflagging fortitude. Some of the descriptions in Acts – here the girl hearing Peter's voice through the door – are so vivid you feel you, too, are there.

Acts 12. 1 – 19 (RSV)
About that time Herod the king laid violent hands upon some who belonged to the church. 2 He killed James the brother of John with the sword; 3 and when he saw that it pleased the Jews, he proceeded to arrest Peter also. This was during the days of Unleavened Bread. 4 And when he had seized him, he put him in prison, and delivered him to four squads of soldiers to guard him, intending after the Passover to bring him out to the people. 5 So Peter was kept in prison; but earnest prayer for him was made to God by the church.

6 The very night when Herod was about to bring him out, Peter was sleeping between two soldiers, bound with two chains, and sentries before the door were guarding the prison; 7 and behold, an angel of

the Lord appeared, and a light shone in the cell; and he struck Peter on the side and woke him, saying, "Get up quickly." And the chains fell off his hands. 8 And the angel said to him, "Dress yourself and put on your sandals." And he did so. And he said to him, "Wrap your mantle around you and follow me." 9 And he went out and followed him; he did not know that what was done by the angel was real, but thought he was seeing a vision. 10 When they had passed the first and the second guard, they came to the iron gate leading into the city. It opened to them of its own accord, and they went out and passed on through one street; and immediately the angel left him. 11 And Peter came to himself, and said, "Now I am sure that the Lord has sent his angel and rescued me from the hand of Herod and from all that the Jewish people were expecting."

12 When he realised this, he went to the house of Mary, the mother of John whose other name was Mark, where many were gathered together and were praying. 13 And when he knocked at the door of the gateway, a maid named Rhoda came to answer. 14 Recognising Peter's voice, in her joy she did not open the gate but ran in and told that Peter was standing at the gate. 15 They said to her, "You are mad." But she insisted that it was so. They said, "It is his angel!" But Peter continued knocking; and when they opened, they saw him and were amazed. 17 But motioning to them with his hand to be silent, he

described to them how the Lord had brought him out of the prison. And he said, "Tell this to James and to the brethren." Then he departed and went to another place.

18 Now when day came, there was no small stir among the soldiers over what had become of Peter. 19 And when Herod had sought for him and could not find him, he examined the sentries and ordered that they should be put to death. Then he went down from Judea to Caesarea, and remained there.

After a year spent working to build up and consolidate the church in Antioch, Paul and Barnabas, supported by their fellow workers, feel called to take the Word to a wider sphere.

Acts 13. 1 – 3 (RSV)
Now in the church at Antioch there were prophets and teachers, Barnabas, Simeon who was called Niger, Lucius of Cyrene, Manaen a member of the court of Herod the tetrarch, and Saul. 2 While they were worshipping the Lord and fasting, the Holy Spirit said, "Set apart for me Barnabas and Saul for the work to which I have called them." 3 Then after fasting and praying they laid their hands on them and sent them off.

So Paul sets out on the start of his incredible journeying and drama-filled life, so vividly described in Acts from chapter 13 onwards. Without having personally met Jesus, the revelation he was granted at his Damascene conversion is enough to drive him relentlessly on in pursuit of a mission that will only end with his imprisonment and death. Together, first with Barnabas, and then, after their sad disagreement, with Silas, Timothy, and others, Paul seeks, in city after city, to proclaim the Good News.

Acts lists 25 places where he preached the message, with implicit revisits required wherever he was successful. At least another 20 places are reported through which he travelled or sailed to, including his shipwreck on Malta (location of his other two shipwrecks are not identified).

Paul and his colleagues follow a set pattern in each city. The obvious place to begin their mission is the local synagogue, the home of the laws and customs which have provided the very starting place for the new faith. This was the place, more than any other, where the message of that new faith should be understood and welcomed.

Perhaps Paul still hoped for true reformation and change of heart in the old establishment. If so, he was due to be disappointed. Often there were those who welcomed the news and put themselves forward for conversion, sometimes in large numbers; but, normally, there were equal or greater numbers who were not convinced, prompting Paul to express frustrated disappointment.

Acts 28. 23 – 28 (RSV)

23 When they had appointed a day for him, they came to him at his lodging in great numbers. And he expounded the matter to them from morning till evening, testifying to the kingdom of God and trying to convince them about Jesus both from the law of Moses and from the prophets. 24 And some were convinced by what he said, while others disbelieved. 25 So as they disagreed among themselves, they departed, after Paul had made one statement: "The Holy Spirit was right in saying to your fathers through Isaiah the prophet:

26 'Go to this people, and say,
You shall indeed hear but never understand,
and you shall indeed see but never perceive,
27 For this people's heart has grown dull
and their ears are heavy of hearing,
and their eyes they have closed;
lest they should perceive with their eyes,
and hear with their ears,
and understand with their heart,
and turn for me to heal them.'

28 Let it be known to you then that this salvation of God has been sent to the Gentiles;

Always their proclamations made a stir, often with trouble attached, with hostile opponents inciting violence and riot. Mostly the opposition was Jewish religious, with indignant Orthodox observers calling for retribution for the heresies they had been obliged to listen to, in particular the outrageous proposition that Gentiles should be admitted to the faithful. Occasionally, though, it originated from tragi-comic economic disruption – Demetrius and the other enraged silversmiths of Ephesus foreseeing the market collapse of one of their most successful lines – silver artefacts relating to the goddess Artemis. Never, it seems, outside the followers, did the peace and love of the message merit a moment's thought. Always it was "These men who have turned the world upside down..."

Acts 17. 6 – 7   (RSV)

6 And when they could not find them, they dragged Jason and some of the brethren before the city authorities, crying, "These men who have turned the world upside down, have come here also, 7 And Jason has received them; and they are all acting against the decrees of Caesar, saying that there is another king, Jesus."

Come what may, Paul continues. How many times were he and his companions arrested, imprisoned, beaten, stoned, plotted against? Always on, on, on with the work.

His attention has to be given, too, to matters outside of carrying the message. The traditional Jewish party, as it were, of the converts has staged a fightback from the defeat they have been forced to concede over taking the Word direct to the Gentiles. "Very well" they say but then they must concede some acknowledgement of the faith's Jewish origins by being, at least, circumcised.

This is against the fundamental principle, held to by Paul, of the equality of all God's creation, apart from it being an apparent sanction against and deterrent to the Gentiles. It must be fought. He goes to Jerusalem, and wins a compromise with a substituted handful of relatively anodyne 'Jewish' recommendations for Christian converts.

Paul returns to Antioch to bring the news of this decision to the Gentiles converted. Then, after the split with Barnabas, he and Silas head through Syria and Galicia, before Derbe, Galatia, Troas, Philippi, Thessalonica, Beroe, Athens, Corinth, Cenchre, Ephesus, Caesarea, back to Antioch, Galatia and Phrygia, Macedonia, Greece, Troas, Tyre, Ptolemais, and Caesaria.

He has been feeling the call for some time to go to Jerusalem again. Everyone advises him against it. He is particularly hated by the Temple authorities there who have converted his victory against circumcision being required for converted Gentiles into an accusation that he frees Jewish converts to Christianity from any requirement to follow the law of Moses. Paul feels that he will have to suffer many tribulations if he goes, but is adamant that he must.

At Jerusalem, the Temple indeed attempts to have him condemned, with the Roman authorities, as a result, getting involved. The Romans perceive Paul as innocent of any punishable offence in their terms, but are anxious not to offend the Jews. The result is interminable Roman custody. Eventually Paul is sent, as a Roman citizen, to Rome for judgement. His 'house arrest-type ' arrangements, however, seem, initially anyway, to be very humane, and Acts ends its account of his story with...

Acts 28. 30 – 31 (RSV)
30 And he lived there two whole years at his own expense, and welcomed all who came to him,   31 preaching the kingdom of God and teaching about the Lord Jesus Christ quite openly and unhindered.

The silence that then follows this statement both from and about him is an indication of his likely death, possibly during the reign of Nero. The chances of his falling foul of the authorities must always have been high.

Letters

of Paul

Chapter XXIII
Paul

When you read about and from Paul, the man that emerges is a phenomenon. That one revelation at Damascus will be enough to drive him relentlessly on, for the rest of his life, to bring the Word he initially persecuted to every corner of the Roman world.

Endlessly he will try, in city after city, to bring to often cynical, indifferent, and often and often actively hostile peoples the revelation he had himself experienced. He will aim to turn their world upside down and then stand alongside them in the struggle to form a community in whose life the message is a true reality.

Then on to a new city; on but never truly leaving behind the places he has left – as revealed in his letters, always in his thoughts, worries, plans. And indeed, how vulnerable those little communities must have been. Anyone who has been part of a local community project knows how fragile they are; how much they depend on strong committed leadership; how easy it is for people to fall away or fall out; how often a venture simply drifts into oblivion. Paul's letters are an attempt, from afar, to sustain, steer, support, encourage, and sometimes severely tell off those little communities for which he felt so responsible.

The pattern he and Barnabas followed in their evangelism reflects their, and the entire Jewish world's belief that theirs was a chosen people who had been 'entrusted with the oracles of God' (Romans 3. 21) to be stewarded and held by them as trustees for the whole world until such time as it was, perhaps, ready to come forward and submit itself to the law of the Judaic religion.

It explains Paul's fanatical, almost, defence of the Jewish law against the aims, as he saw them then, of the 'Nazarene Sect'. Once convinced that Christ's message was, in fact, the ultimate and true fulfilment of that law, he felt the same driving obligation to bring about its replacement of the old establishment he had once so fiercely defended. To the local synagogue, then, he and Barnabas would go as soon as they entered a new town to attempt to persuade the Jews that they bore the call, from the Messiah they had all been waiting for, for the regeneration of his church. As Jesus, himself, had originally thought, the message was destined, first, for them.

As described earlier, any hopes they had for a general acceptance by the faithful were due to be disappointed. Usually there were converts, some-times in large numbers, but there were also the unconvinced, scoffers, and, often also in large numbers, outraged faithful reacting to the message with the same violent hostility that Paul himself had once shown. They could be welcomed into the homes of locals eager to hear more, and preach daily to large numbers, or they could be abused, beaten, arrested, or driven from the town, – sometimes a mixture of all three.

Often referred to as mixed into the group were 'Greeks'. Perhaps 'Greeks' was a term used in designation of Gentiles in general, but, from their heritage of Greek colonies, Greeks must, likely, have been spread more widely across the ancient world than even Jews. Even if not converted to Judaism the synagogue was perhaps one of the few places locally they could count on getting the intellectual stimulus they prized. Numbers of these are reported also as converts – the growing presence of the Gentiles.

From what Paul, himself, says, it would appear he was not a natural, magnetic speaker. His proclamation of the message must have been backed by the sheer force of his conviction, the example of his amazing story, and what must have been the power of his extraordinary personality.

As the resistance and rejection element in the synagogues continued, in contrast with the often eager welcome the teachings received among non-Jewish audiences, the conviction gradually took hold that perhaps the message was also destined to go straight, as it was, not through the medium of the Jewish law, on an equal footing, to the Gentile world.

Even when this startling concept had been fairly generally accepted, it was still assumed by many Jews converted via the Judaic law route that Gentiles' introduction to the new faith would involve them, first, in some retrospective submission to Jewish law and ritual e.g. circumcision. In due course this requirement came under sharper and sharper scrutiny. Why should a non-Jewish person who had just given over their life to the deep faith of Christ's teaching now need to subject themselves to a, from their point of view, completely unconnected and alien, painful, physical ordeal?

It was clear to Paul that this could not continue, but his dispensing of this need caused huge upheavals. To many Jewish Christians, the idea that they could find themselves shoulder to shoulder with fellow Christians whose route to the faith had been entirely independent of Jewish law and ritual was impossible to accept. It was taken by many as an indication that the faith, as promoted by Paul, was aiming for the destruction of the law of Moses, with Paul's consequent vilification.

Eventually Paul felt he must submit the issue to Jerusalem and the authority there made unique by the still living disciples who had personally associated with Jesus. In an endearingly human conclusion, the council there fully endorsed the principle of the divorce between adoption of the Christian faith and compliance with Jewish law, as exemplified in circumcision, but shrank from complete disconnection between the two, by proposing that Gentile converts should commit themselves only to observance of a couple of the milder dietary requirements of Jewish law – for example, abstaining from eating meat that had been strangled.

Backsliding on this forward-thinking concession, however, would repeatedly continue. Again and again Paul would need to contradict stricter dietary requirements laid on new Gentile converts, and stirrings of the 'circumcision party'.

The Jews were deeply reluctant to give up their stewardship responsibilities for the 'oracles of God'. Even Peter and Paul, himself, succumbed at times to 'circumcision party' pressures, to avoid getting, otherwise, sidetracked into endless sterile dispute, upheaval, and genuine distress from sincere, good, Jewish Christians who also sincerely held to the need for Judaic law. Paul castigates Peter for behaving equivocally in respect of Jewish dietary requirements.

Galatians 2. 11- 12   (RSV)
11   But when Cephas came to Antioch I opposed him to his face, because he stood condemned.   12 For before certain men came from James, he ate

with the Gentiles; but when they came he drew back and separated himself, fearing the circumcision party.

Yet Paul himself then proceeds to make an even more drastic concession to the controversy to ensure that his companion evangelist will not be dismissed by Jewish listeners before he even opens his mouth.

Acts 16. 1 – 3 (RSV)

And he came also to Derbe and to Lystra. A disciple was there, named Timothy, the son of a Jewish woman who was a believer; but his father was a Greek. 2 He was well spoken of by the brethren at Lystra and Iconium. 3 Paul wanted Timothy to accompany him; and he took him and circumcised him because of the Jews that were in those places, for they all knew that his father was a Greek.

Chapter XXIV
The new communities

There was so much to worry about in relation to the new convert communities. How was their faith faring in the wear and tear of daily life now that the first excitement of conversion was over? Were they transcending the inevitable disagreements and jealousies that arose in every community, and not succumbing to petty rivalries such as the Corinthians apparently had (1 Corinthians 1 10 – 17) over who had been the instrument of their conversion – "I was baptised by Paul", "But I was baptised by Apollos" - rivalries as silly as they were also fraught with dangerous cult potential.

Were they respecting the right of Gentile converts not to conform to Judaic law and practices? Were they facing hostility and intimidation from outside, and, if so, how were they standing up to it? Were they continuing to follow the true path and not wandering off or being led astray onto false trails?

Paul attempts to address these concerns in his letters, normally with a beginning of fulsome encouragement and praise for the reports he has had of the community, followed by a stream of, as appropriate, exhortations, advice, strictures (sometimes severe), admonitions and urgings, with, in their midst, like shafts from the great pool of sunlight that obviously lay at the core of his faith.

Romans 8. 35 – 39   (RSV)

35 Who shall separate us from the love of Christ? Shall tribulation, or distress, or persecution, or famine, or nakedness, or peril, or sword? 36 As it is written

"For thy sake we are being killed all the day long; we are regarded as sheep to be slaughtered."

37 No, in all these things we are more than conquerors through him who loved us. 38 For I am sure that neither death, nor life, nor angels, nor principalities, nor things present, nor things to come, nor powers, 39 nor height, nor depth, nor anything else in all creation will be able to separate us from the love of God in Christ Jesus our Lord.

Galatians 5. 14 (RSV)

14 For the whole law is fulfilled in one word, "You shall love your neighbour as yourself."

Then his wonderful treatise on how we are all interdependent on each other and part of the same enterprise.

1 Corinthians 12. 4 – 30   (RSV)

4   Now there are varieties of gifts, but the same Spirit. 5   and there are varieties of service, but the same Lord; 6 and there are varieties of working, but it is the same God who inspires them all in everyone. 7 To each is given the manifestation of the Spirit for the common good. 8   To one is given through the Spirit the utterance of wisdom, and to another the utterance of knowledge according to the same Spirit, 9 to another faith by the same Spirit, to another gifts of healing by the one Spirit,   10   to another the working of miracles, to another prophecy, to another the ability to distinguish between spirits, to another various   kinds   of   tongues,   to   another   the interpretation of tongues. 11 All these are inspired by one and the same Spirit, who apportions to each one individually as he wills.

12   For just as the body is one and has many members, and all the members of the body, though many, are one body, so it is with Christ. 13 For by one Spirit we were all baptised into one body – Jews or Greeks, slaves or free – and all were made to drink of one Spirit.

14 For the body does not consist of one member, 15 If the foot should say, "Because I am not a hand, I do not belong to the body," that would not make it any less a part of the body.   16   And if the ear should say, "Because I am not an eye, I do not belong to the body," that would not make it any less

a part of the body. 17 If the whole body were an eye, where would be the hearing? If the whole body were an ear, where would be the sense of smell? 18 But as it is, God arranged the organs in the body of each one of them, as he chose. 19 If all were a single organ, where would the body be? 20 As it is, there are many parts, yet one body. 21 The eye cannot say to the hand, "I have no need of you," 22 On the contrary, the parts of the body which seem to be weaker are indispensable, 23 and those parts of the body which we think less honourable we invest with the greater honour, and our unpresentable parts are treated with greater modesty, 24 which our more presentable parts do not require. But God has so composed the body, giving the greater honour to the inferior part, 25 that there may be no discord in the body, but that the members may have the same care for one another. 26 If one member suffers, all suffer together; if one member is honoured, all rejoice together.

27   Now you are the body of Christ and individually members of it.   28 And God has appointed in the church first apostles, second prophets, third teachers, then workers of miracles, then healers, helpers, administrators, speakers in various kinds of tongues. 29 Are all apostles? Are all prophets? Are all teachers? Do all work miracles? 30 Do all possess gifts of healing? Do all speak with tongues? Do all interpret?

... and ending with his glorious declaration – the litmus test of whether something is of God or not.

1 Corinthians 13. 1 – 13 (RSV)

If I speak in the tongues of men and of angels, but have not love, I am a noisy gong or a clanging cymbal. 2 And if I have prophetic powers, and understand all mysteries and all knowledge, and if I have all faith, so as to remove mountains, but have not love, I am nothing. 3 If I give away all I have, and if I deliver my body to be burned, but have not love, I gain nothing.

4 Love is patient and kind; love is not jealous or boastful; 5 it is not arrogant or rude. Love does not insist on its own way; it is not irritable or resentful; 6 it does not rejoice at wrong, but rejoices in the right. 7 Love bears all things, believes all things, hopes all things, endures all things.

8 Love never ends; as for prophecies, they will pass away; as for tongues, they will cease; as for knowledge, it will pass away. 9 For our knowledge is imperfect and our prophecy is imperfect; 10 but when the perfect comes, the imperfect will pass away.

11 When I was a child, I spoke like a child, I thought like a child, I reasoned like a child; when I became a man, I gave up childish ways. 12 For now we see in a mirror dimly, but then face to face. Now I know in part; then I shall understand fully,

even as I have been fully understood. 13 So faith, hope, love abide, these three; but the greatest of these is love.

Paul's greatest worry seems to have centred on self-appointed teachers with their own, and, Paul fears, maybe false, take on the Christian message, leading communities away from the teachings which he had laid before them.

He was so convinced that his interpretations of the message were the truest and best way to come to Christ that he launches into competitive self-promotion to convince his readers that they gained nothing from going elsewhere, a comic element in himself that he was aware of and endearingly acknowledged even as he beat his drum.

2 Corinthians 11. 1 – 6 (RSV)

I wish you would bear with me in a little foolishness. Do bear with me! 2 I feel a divine jealousy for you, for I betrothed you to Christ to present you as a pure bride to her one husband. 3 But I am afraid that as the serpent deceived Eve by his cunning, your thoughts will be led astray from a sincere and pure devotion to Christ. 4 For if some one comes and preaches another Jesus than the one we preached, or if you receive a different spirit from the one you received, or if you accept a different gospel from the one you accepted, you submit to it readily enough. 5

I think that I am not in the least inferior to these
superlative apostles. 6   Even if I am unskilled in
speaking, I am not in knowledge; in every way we
have made this plain to you in all things.

And the catalogue of what he has submitted himself
to.

2 Corinthians 11. 21 – 28   (RSV)

21 … But whatever anyone dares to boast of – I am
speaking as a fool – I also dare to boast of that. 22
Are they Hebrews? So am I. Are they Israelites? So
am I. Are they descendants of Abraham? So am I.
23 Are they servants of Christ? I am a better one – I
am talking like a madman – with far greater labours,
far more imprisonments, with countless beatings,
and often near death. 24 Five times I have received
at the hands of the Jews the forty lashes less one.
25 Three times I have been beaten with rods; once I
was stoned. Three times I have been shipwrecked; a
night and a day I have been adrift at sea; 26   on
frequent journeys, in danger from rivers, danger from
robbers, danger from my own people, danger from
Gentiles, danger in the city, danger in the
wilderness, danger at sea, danger from false
brethren; 27 in toil and hardship, through many a
sleepless night, in hunger and thirst, often without
food, in cold and exposure. 28   And, apart from
other things, there is the daily pressure upon me of

my anxiety for all the churches.

I wonder at what point I might have felt entitled to tread a little more softly?

A member of an established religion today has the option to drop off the vehicle for a time, to consider where they stand, to take time out, to award themselves some self-indulgence, and then, when they feel ready, to hop back on again, safe in the certainty that someone, somewhere, in the church established, will have kept the momentum of the heart of the message going.

Paul and his colleagues had no such luxury. They were, essentially, the momentum, the keepers of the treasure, without whom the great venture could peter out, stagnate, or drift off onto an unrelated tack. They had to be permanently on their guard and at their posts, and ready to address any aspect of living the faith in a Christian community, whether fundamental faith questions, practical issues, or simple administration (see Paul's instructions on appointing elders)

1 Timothy 3. 1 – 13   (RSV)
The saying is sure: If any one aspires to the office of bishop, he desires a noble task. 2 Now a bishop must be above reproach, the husband of one wife, temperate, sensible, dignified, hospitable, an apt teacher, 3 no drunkard, not violent but gentle, not

quarrelsome, and no lover of money. 4 He must manage his own household well, keeping his children submissive and respectful in every way; 5 for if a man does not know how to manage his own household, how can he care for God's church? 6 He must not be a recent convert, or he may be puffed up with conceit and fall into the condemnation of the devil; 7 moreover he must be well thought of by outsiders, or he may fall into reproach and the snare of the devil.

8 Deacons likewise must be serious, not double-tongued, not addicted to much wine, not greedy for gain; 9 they must hold the mystery of the faith with a clear conscience. 10 And let them also be tested first; then, if they prove themselves blameless let them serve as deacons. 11 The women likewise must be serious, no slanderers, but temperate, faithful in all things. 12 Let deacons be the husband of one wife, and let them manage their children and their households well; 13 for those who serve well as deacons gain a good standing for themselves and also great confidence in the faith which is in Christ Jesus.

...and his statement of a rule of life (the ancestor of the Desiderata?)...

Romans 12. 9 – 21   (RSV)
9 Let love be genuine; hate what is evil, hold fast to

what is good; 10 love one another with brotherly affection; outdo one another in showing honour. 11 Never flag in zeal, be aglow with the Spirit, serve the Lord. 12 Rejoice in your hope, be patient in tribulation, be constant in prayer. 13 Contribute to the needs of the saints, practise hospitality.

14 Bless those who persecute you; bless and do not curse them. 15 Rejoice with those who rejoice, weep with those who weep. 16 Live in harmony with one another; do not be haughty, but associate with the lowly; never be conceited. 17 Repay no one evil for evil, but take thought for what is noble in the sight of all. 18 If possible, so far as it depends on you, live peaceably with all. 19 Beloved, never avenge yourselves, but leave it to the wrath of God; for it is written, "Vengeance is mine, I will repay, says the Lord". 20 No, "if your enemy is hungry, feed him; if he is thirsty, give him drink; for by so doing you will heap burning coals upon his head". Do not be overcome by evil but overcome evil with good.

Chapter XXV
Empty vessels

I am greatly heartened by Paul's reference to "the folly of what we preach". Nothing less would be relevant to engage with the life of our human world.

1 Corinthians 1. 21 (RSV)
21 For since, in the wisdom of God, the world did not know God through wisdom, it pleased God through the folly of what we preach to save those who believe.

I am greatly encouraged, too, by one of Paul's refrains, that God constantly works in and through our weakness. It means nothing is irrelevant, nothing is futile. God only needs vessels. If we are simply there, available to Him, he doesn't need our *help as well*!

I am reminded of a time I was hospital visiting, an activity I, on the whole, feel pretty uncomfortable with, being fundamentally shy and short on confidence. I had gone up to a bed where the occupant, a man, was lying turned away from me towards the wall, not moving. It was not possible to tell whether he was asleep. It was a moot point whether I should just move on, but somehow it didn't seem quite good enough.

"Hello," I said launching into the dreaded opening gambit. "I'm Michael, a volunteer from the chaplaincy downstairs. How are you today?"

No movement, a pause, and then an inaudible mumble of a couple of words. Already I'd run out of options! I'm screaming in my head to leave.

"Have you been in long?" I say.

Again a pause and then another inaudible mutter.

"Well I'll leave you to rest. I hope you're soon out of here."

Then low, but clear: "Don't go."

"What?" I said startled.

Again: "Don't go."

All he wanted was the company of another human being with him.

I wish I could say I spent the next half-hour just sitting with him, perhaps holding his hand if he wished it, but I can't. My obsessive focus on how *I* felt, uncomfortable with the situation not conforming to the chatting scenario *I* felt appropriate, meant that, flustered by this unplanned proposal, I said: "Well I'll stay for a few more minutes and then I'll have to go".

And that is what I did, something I still vehemently kick myself about when I think of it.

And further, in the situation of experiencing

weakness, we have Paul's inspirational description of the 'thorn in the flesh' he came to suffer, not gladly, and his prayers to the Lord that he be freed of it, before realising that what he lost of himself through this suffering created the need and the opportunity for Christ to come and fill that space in him.

2 Corinthians 12. 7 – 10   (RSV)
7   And to keep me from being too elated by the abundance of revelations, a thorn was given me in the flesh, a messenger from Satan, to harass me, to keep me from being too elated. 8   Three times I besought the Lord about this, that it should leave me: 9 but he said to me, "My grace is sufficient for you, for my power is made perfect in weakness." I will all the more gladly boast of my weaknesses, that the power of Christ may rest upon me. 10 For the sake of Christ, then, I am content with weaknesses, insults, hardships, persecutions, and calamities; for when I am weak, then I am strong.

We are so used to think of Paul as indomitable, that it is a moving and deeply impressive surprise when one reads the feelings he was experiencing, which he sometimes shared in his correspondence.

2 Corinthians 1. 8 (RSV)
8 For we do not want you to be ignorant, brethren, of the affliction we experienced in Asia; for we were

so utterly, unbearably crushed that we despaired of life itself.

It is clear also that his later proper imprisonment was a great burden of suffering to him which he often refers to.

2 Timothy 2. 8 – 9   (RSV)
8 Remember Jesus Christ, risen from the dead, descended from David, as preached in my gospel, 9 the gospel for which I am suffering and wearing fetters like a criminal.

1 Thessalonians 3. 7 (RSV)
7   For this reason, brethren, in all our distress and affliction we have been comforted about you through your faith;

Colossians 4. 18   (RSV)
18   I, Paul, write this greeting with my own hand. Remember my fetters. Grace be with you.

But even there, blessings were to be found...

Philippians 1. 12 – 14   (RSV)
12   I want you to know, brethren, that what has happened to me has really served to advance the gospel, 13 so that it has become known throughout the whole praetorian guard and to all the rest that my

imprisonment is for Christ;   14   and most of the brethren have been made confident in the Lord because of my imprisonment, and are much more bold to speak the word of God without fear.

And he refers later to the saints from 'Caesar's household'.

Paul was obviously a man with very strong views, with some of which, in company of numerous other people, I take issue. In particular his views, the absolute norms, I am sure, for the day, on the role of women in society, and on homosexuality.

I also find baffling the focus he gives to condemning and combating sex for sex's sake. While most people, I think, would agree that unbridled licentiousness, persistently pursued, is not only sterile, but probably destructive to all parties involved, I find I put a little lustful naughtiness fairly low on the list of human heinousness, with cruelty, oppression, exploitation, and neglect in a different league.

The only explanation I can give myself is that Paul's aim was for all his converts to experience what he, himself, was experiencing – that is, it is my belief, to love God with all his heart, and with all his soul, and with all his mind, and all his strength, and that it was Pauline impatience with what he perceived as the greatest and most common distraction among his charges from pursuing that aim, common or garden sex, that made him fulminate so strongly against it. In Ephesians 1, he expresses his vision of what life is about.

Ephesians 1. 3 – 14 (RSV)

3 Blessed be the God and Father of our lord Jesus Christ, who has blessed us in Christ with every spiritual blessing in the heavenly places, 4 even as he chose us in him before the foundation of the world, that we should be holy and blameless before him. 5 He destined us in love to be his sons through Jesus Christ, according to the purpose of his will, 6 to the praise of his glorious grace which he freely bestowed on us in the Beloved. 7 In him we have redemption through his blood, the forgiveness of our trespasses, according to the riches of his grace 8 which he lavished upon us. 9 For he has made known to us in all wisdom and insight the mystery of his will, according to his purpose which he set forth in Christ 10 as a plan for the fullness of time, to unite all things in him, things in heaven and things on earth.

11 In him, according to the purpose of him who accomplishes all things according to the counsel of his will, 12 we who first hoped in Christ have been destined and appointed to live for the praise of his glory. 13 In him you also, who have heard the word of truth, the gospel of your salvation, and have believed in him, were sealed with the promised Holy

Spirit, 14 which is the guarantee of our inheritance until we acquire possession of it to the praise of his glory.

The indications are also that he, in common with other apostles and disciples, may still have been thinking of the second coming as imminent. Time was short. If you were serious about your beliefs you had to get on with it.

Paul, celibate himself, would wish that others would follow his example and give their full attention to what mattered, but he acknowledges also less disciplined human nature, and if you have to have space for sex, then accommodate it in an appropriate form.

Romans 6. 12 – 14   (RSV)
12 Let not sin therefore reign in your mortal bodies, to make you obey their passions. 13 Do not yield your members to sin as instruments of wickedness, but yield yourselves to God as men who have been brought from death to life, and your members to God as instruments of righteousness. 14 For sin will have no dominion over you, since you are not under law but under grace.

Romans 8. 5 – 6 (RSV)
5 For those who live according to the flesh set their minds on the things of the flesh but those who live

according to the Spirit set their minds on the things of the Spirit. 6 To set the mind on the flesh is death, but to set the mind on the Spirit is life and peace.

1 Corinthians 7. 1 – 9   (RSV)

Now concerning the matters about which you wrote. It is well for a man not to touch a woman. 2 But because of the temptation to immorality, each man should have his own wife and each woman her own husband. 3 The husband should give to his wife her conjugal rights, and likewise the wife to her husband. 4 For the wife does not rule over her own body, but the husband does; likewise the husband does not rule over his own body but the wife does. 5 Do not refuse one another except perhaps by agreement for a season, that you may devote yourselves to prayer; but then come together again, lest Satan tempt you through lack of self-control. 6 I say this by way of concession, not of command. 7 I wish that all were as I myself am. But each has his own special gift from God, one of one kind and one of another.

8 To the unmarried and the widows I say that it is well for them to remain single as I do. 9 But if they cannot exercise self-control, they should marry. For it is better to marry than to be aflame with passion.

1 Corinthians 7. 25 – 38(RSV)

25   Now concerning the unmarried, I have no command of the Lord, but I give my opinion as one

who by the Lord's mercy is trustworthy. 26 I think that in view of the present distress it is well for a person to remain as he is. 27 Are you bound to a wife? Do not seek to be free. Are you free from a wife? Do not seek marriage. 28 But if you marry, you do not sin, and if a girl marries she does not sin. Yet those who marry will have worldly troubles, and I would spare you that. 29 I mean, brethren, the appointed time has grown very short; from now on, let those who have wives live as though they had none, 30 and those who mourn as though they were not mourning, and those who rejoice as though they were not rejoicing, and those who buy as though they had no goods, 31 and those who deal with the world as though they had no dealings with it. For the form of this world is passing away.

32 I want you to be free from anxieties. The unmarried man is anxious about the affairs of the Lord, how to please the Lord; 33 but the married man is anxious about worldly affairs, how to please his wife, 34 and his interests are divided. And the unmarried woman or girl is anxious about the affairs of the Lord, how to be holy in body and spirit; but the married woman is anxious about worldly affairs, how to please her husband. 35 I say this for your own benefit, not to lay any restraint upon you, but to promote good order and to secure your undivided devotion to the Lord.

36 If anyone thinks that he is not behaving

properly towards his betrothed, if his passions are strong, and it has to be, let him do as he wishes: let them marry – it is no sin. 37 But whoever is firmly established in his heart, being under no necessity but having his desire under control, and has determined this in his heart, to keep her as his betrothed, he will do well. 38 So that he who marries his betrothed does well; and he who refrains from marriage will do better.

Galatians 5. 16 – 24 (RSV)
16 But I say, walk by the Spirit, and do not gratify the desires of the flesh. 17 For the desires of the flesh are against the Spirit, and the desires of the Spirit are against the flesh; for these are opposed to each other, to prevent you from doing what you would. 18 But if you are led by the Spirit you are not under the law. 19 Now the works of the flesh are plain: fornication, impurity, licentiousness, 20 idolatry, sorcery, enmity, strife, jealousy, anger, selfishness, dissension, party spirit, 21 envy, drunkenness, carousing, and the like. I warn you, as I warned you before, that those who do such things shall not inherit the kingdom of God. 22 But the fruit of the Spirit is love, joy, peace, patience, kindness, goodness, faithfulness, 23 gentleness, self-control; against such there is no law. 24 And those who belong to Christ Jesus have crucified the flesh with its passions and desires.

25 If we live by the Spirit, let us also walk by the Spirit.

The perceived shortness of time explains also Paul's, otherwise apparently rather un-Christian, urgings to have nothing to do with those not subscribing to the new faith or not living in accordance with it.

2 Corinthians 6. 14   (RSV)
14 Do not be mismated with unbelievers. For what partnership have righteousness and iniquity? Or what fellowship has light with darkness?

2 Thessalonians 3. 6   (RSV)
6 Now we command you, brethren, in the name of our lord Jesus Christ, that you keep away from any brother who is living in idleness and not in accord with the tradition that you received from us.

There wasn't time to bring everyone into the fold. Converts must concentrate first on perfecting their own relationship with God. His compassion is still there, however, for those who fall by the wayside.

Galatians 6. 1 – 2 (RSV)
Brethren, if a man is overtaken in any trespass, you who are spiritual should restore him in a spirit of gentleness. Look to yourself, lest you too be tempted.. 2 Bear one another's burdens, and so

fulfil the law of Christ.

On authority, also, I see the same pattern. Whatever
his views on slavery (it is impossible to imagine Paul
'owning' anyone), the first call of the faith was union
with God. Achievement of that would bring the
inevitable resolution of all social issues (see
Colossians 3.11 - 'Here there cannot be Greek and
Jew, circumcised and uncircumcised, barbarian,
Scythian, slave, free man...'); but if slavery was
abolished without the achievement of union with
God, the mission, as far as Paul was concerned,
would have been a failure.

I finish with his encouragement...

2 Thessalonians 3. 13   (RSV)
13 Brethren, do not be weary in well-doing.

And his really very excellent recommendation...

Philippians 4. 8 – 9 (RSV)
8   Finally, brethren, whatever is true, whatever is
honourable, whatever is just, whatever is pure,
whatever is lovely, whatever is gracious, if there is
any excellence, if there is anything worthy of praise,
think about these things. 9 What you have learned
and received and heard and seen in me, do; and the
God of peace will be with you.

Epilogue

I acknowledge that what follows below is inspired entirely by a short story someone told me of, about a religious sceptic who manages to create an H. G. Wells-type machine to travel back to the time of Christ to settle the question once and for all: a story I never managed to locate in the original, or identify the author of.

In my much less radical version the hero, Martin, succeeds in travelling to the Holy Land around the year AD 31. He stops the first person he meets and asks for Jesus. Unhesitatingly the man directs him to the Temple. There, outside, he finds a huge crowd gathered round a Jesus-looking figure, who is laying his hands on a succession of people lined up to see him. From their reaction afterwards it appears that these people are receiving healing, or imagine they are.

Martin pushes through the crowd to the front to get a better view. Two things immediately strike him. Jesus appears to be totally silent. He simply lays his hands on each person brought to him and then waits for the next. The other thing is that although there are a few rather anonymous-looking individuals near Jesus who might be disciples, they are also silent and play no part in the proceedings.

The people who dominate the scene and bring forward those who have come to be healed are scribes and Pharisees from the Temple. At each successful healing they turn to address the crowd calling on them to acknowledge the power of God of which they have been designated the curators on earth.

Some people they turn away, whom Martin is convinced the Jesus of the New Testament would have seen, denouncing them as sinners and outcasts. Jesus shows no reaction to what they do. He appears oblivious to everything around him. Eventually the healing is over. The crowd disperses, the scribes and Pharisees go back to the Temple, and Jesus and the anonymous-looking associates melt away into the city.

Next day, and each day after, Martin follows the crowds that make their way to Jesus, in many different places. Where he goes appears to be the only decision Jesus takes independently of the Temple. Each day it is the same; a huge crowd and a long line of people who have come to be healed, who are sorted, selected, or turned away by the scribes and Pharisees, the lucky ones brought forward to a silent Jesus for him to lay hands on. Each successful healing is followed by a short discourse from the Pharisees to the crowd.

Martin finds himself getting increasingly agitated.

All of the people turned away, he is convinced, would have been welcomed by the Jesus of the New Testament. Many of the pronouncements made by the scribes and Pharisees on the back of the successful healings are also in direct contradiction of the teachings in the Gospels.

Then, one day, the location chosen by Jesus is indoors. The place is packed. Martin hardly manages to push in. He notices there are no scribes and Pharisees present. A line of people are already forming for Jesus when suddenly there is a great commotion and a large body of scribes and Pharisees force their way through the crowd to the front. At that moment a shaft of sunlight floods into the room, as slates are removed from above, and the next minute a pallet is being lowered from the roof with a paralysed man on it. At once the Pharisees swing into action.

"He will not heal today," calls out the leader. "It is the sabbath.

"You have already broken the Sabbath," he shouts up to those on the roof. "Take him away now and come back to the Temple for repentance for yourselves."

Those above appear to hesitate and then reluctantly start to pull up the ropes.

"No!" shouts Martin, fighting his way to the front. "He wishes to heal him."

The scribes and Pharisees swing round in

disbelief.

"Who dares to question the authority of the Temple?" roars the leader. "We are his chosen voice"

"He wishes to heal him," shouts Martin back.

"Let us see," cries a voice from the crowd. "Let us see what he does."

The cry is taken up. "Let him decide. Let him decide."

The Pharisees are cowed. A deathly hush falls. The paralysed man on the pallet is lowered again to the floor. Jesus appears to have been oblivious of everything, but as the pallet reaches the ground his attention suddenly seems drawn to it. He steps forward and holds his hands above the man.

"He says: 'Man, your sins are forgiven you'," shouts Martin.

The man stands up and picks up his pallet. Uproar breaks out.

Each day, from then on, the crowd turns to Martin to interpret Jesus' silence. He does so, quoting from Jesus' words in the New Testament, constantly contradicting the Pharisees' pronouncements. They are powerless to prevent him. Gradually from being a favoured client Jesus changes for them, from the words put into his mouth, into a mortal enemy threatening their position and very existence.

Finally, they use Martin to provide them with the evidence they need to rid themselves of this thorn in their flesh. "I adjure you," says the High Priest to Jesus, "by the living God, tell us if you are the Christ, the Son of God."

"What does he say?" the High Priest asks Martin.

"He says: 'You have said so'," answers Martin. "But he tells you, hereafter you will see the Son of man seated at the right hand of Power, and coming on the clouds of heaven."

Eventually, Martin travels back to his own time. He simply could not allow Christ's message and his sacrifice not to have taken place.

The Real Press

If you enjoyed this book, please post a review – it makes a huge difference to small publishers. Also, why not take a look at the other books we have on our list at www.therealpress.co.uk ...?

Including the new Armada novel with a difference, *Tearagh't*, by the maverick psychologist Craig Newnes.

Or the medieval thriller *Regicide*, by David Boyle, and introducing Peter Abelard as the great detective...

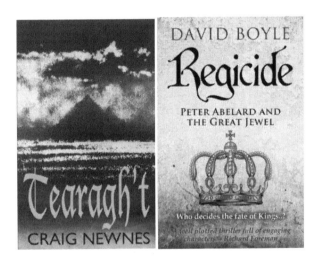

Printed in Great Britain
by Amazon